A Gospel Story

A Journey from Legalism
to the Message of Righteousness by Faith

by Jennifer Jill Schwirzer
Michael Ministries
www.jenniferjill.org

Edited by Madeline Johnston
Cover photo by David Charles Asscherick
Cover model Kimberly Dawn Schwirzer
Graphic design by Caleb VinCross

Unless otherwise indicated, Scripture references are taken from the
New American Standard Bible.

Endnotes are from E.G. White unless otherwise noted.

ISBN 978-0-615-30434-2

Table of Contents

Chapter One
Goody Two-shoes

I converted to Christianity at nineteen years of age. A born-again believer, I set out to find a church that could answer my many burning questions about life, death, love, God, and the way He wanted me to live. Nine months later I was a baptized Seventh-day Adventist.

What you are about to read is an account of a soul's journey through ten years of Adventist experience. Encapsulated within that story is a journey through legalism to righteousness by faith. My burden in this book is not to present the doctrines of the church, although I believe them and wouldn't be a member if I didn't.[1] My burden is to convey a spiritual transition I made within my faith experience, and the message that accompanied that transition. Although the unique features of Adventism will emerge, the story will be relevant to those of other denominations.

My early associates were primarily young, idealistic believers, many newly converted like me, who were quite enthusiastic about Adventist doctrine and lifestyle. I liked the revolutionary flavor of it all—the willingness to be different, the radical departure from accepted norms. Unfortunately (or maybe fortunately—you'll see why), there was a degree of legalism present which colored my experience. When I say "legalism," I mean a focus on the imperatives of the gospel (what we should do) to the exclusion of the declaratives of the gospel (what God has done). The natural results of this are many: a very rigid form of obedience, an effort to save oneself through that obedience, and a disposition to lord all of this over others. I could go on . . .

The sheer energy of untempered idealism swept me away. I loved Jesus, I was deeply converted, but I began to pride myself on my high standards in contrast to other Christians. I was like the Galatian goody-goodies who had "begun in the spirit," but thought they were "being perfected by the flesh." Fortunately, the legalistic period of my life had a function. Goody Two-shoes was "kept in custody under the law, being shut up to the faith which was later to be revealed" (Galatians 3:23). For a time the standards were my safety zone, the rules and regulations my righteousness, but I was "shut up," or reserved, for something that would be revealed . . . "later."

God allowed me to try to earn salvation in order to find out that I never could.

God allowed me to exhaust the possibilities of human effort before He brought me face to face with the truth of righteousness by faith.

Legalism comes easily to Adventists. We teach more specifically on doctrine and lifestyle standards than most Christian religions. This can be traced to the writings of Ellen White, a woman believed to have possessed the gift of prophecy. Although she died in 1915, she lives on in the form of the 25 million words she wrote on subjects ranging from end-time events to Christology to practical living. I have read most of those words and believe she passes the Biblical tests of a true prophet.[2] Conservative Adventists greatly respect and follow her counsels to degrees ranging from principalized to highly literal. In other words, some take the essence of her writing and apply it to present circumstances, but a few apply her counsels too rigidly, with no adaptation to time, culture, and situation. This was my early Adventist leaning. Like many young zealots, I was both optimistic and naïve. Too young to be fettered by the sobering realities of life, I ventured forth to become the model of literal, exact obedience.

Of course, none of us operates in a vacuum, so I must acknowledge that I was influenced heavily by peers. The crowd I ran with focused intensely upon the counsel Ellen White gave on lifestyle and behavioral matters. This involved simple, clean living: a plant-based diet, abstinence from caffeine and nicotine; exercise; and modest, healthy dress, to name a few of the "counsels." We took pride in being very fastidious in obedience. And this was good for the most part. Unfortunately for me, this mentality was taken to what I thought was the next level, leading me to develop a case of anorexia nervosa. If avoiding high-fat, refined foods was good, then avoiding caloric food was better. If grains and beans enhanced spirituality, dry salad made one a saint—at least these were my subconscious reasonings. Soon I weighed 95 pounds (I'm 5'6") and could use my ribs to shelve small objects.

Candidly, the eating disorder became my defense against the sense of condemnation I felt in the presence of the apparently holy people that surrounded me. In my subconscious, my semi-starvation atoned for the sins of past, pre-Christian hedonism. Like a monk, I tried to substitute physical deprivation for true spiritual cleansing. But what looked like extreme devotion was really complacency. A false sense of victory lessened my sense of need of Christ's righteousness.

Such hypervigilance affected all areas of life. I sewed strips of fabric around the bottom of my already long dresses to avoid revealing my spindly legs. Thinking my long hair might be immodest, I wore it pinned up for so long that I developed a bald spot. Rail-thin, well-covered and balding, I was a model of self-flagellation.[3]

You may be tempted to blame Ellen White or Adventist standards for my fanaticism. Please consider the possibility that it's not really about Ellen White or Adventism, but the deeper issues of law and grace. Think of the non-Christian religions; because they are manmade and flow out of the dictates of human nature, they all rest on a foundation of salvation by works. That same human nature can import subtle forms of salvation by works into Christianity. Therefore, Christians of all denominations can fall into the trap of thinking that their obedience saves them. This premise will lead people to shrink the law into a manageable size—typically a list of concrete, externalized behaviors.

My early "can-do" mentality, as impressive as it may have been, betrayed a certain ignorance of the frailty of human flesh. Soon enough, though, I'd confront my need. I think God probably looked down on me at this stage of my life and smiled, saying, "She'll learn." Then He put into motion events that would lead me straight into a brick wall.

That brick wall came while my husband and I worked with a health ministry in New York City. Comprised of a team of young people in our twenties, we operated a vegetarian restaurant in Manhattan, where we served healthful meals to upwards of five hundred people a day. Electrified by the sheer energy and chic of the financial district, and thrilled with the faith-sharing opportunities and each other's company, our little army of twenty-five or so young people marched into Manhattan day after day, filled with the spirit of mission. We were brimming with energy—and hormones. How could a group of young people escape the temptations all around? Not being adequately grounded in the gospel, we relied heavily on bits and bridles.

As the group dynamics progressed, bits and bridles began to break. For instance, the rules of modesty were so exacting that I was rebuked for wearing things like nylon stockings (instead of opaque tights), culottes (it's hard to ride a bike in a long dress), and elbow length sleeves (those tantalizing elbows!). Yet in the midst of all this exactitude there was rampant adultery on the part of the leader and those who succumbed to him. This charismatic man preached purity as feverishly as he sullied it. He loved long, drab dresses on women—and off them, crumbled on the floor at the foot of his adulterous bed. You get the picture—it's the same one Jesus painted with the words, "Woe to you, scribes and Pharisees, hypocrites! For you are like whitewashed tombs which on the outside appear beautiful, but inside they are full of dead men's bones and all uncleanness" (Matthew 23:27). An outsider looking on would have been utterly baffled by the power this man continued to exercise over his minions even after his sexual misconduct became known. Such is the irrationality of Phariseeism, and the reason why Jesus rebuked it so publicly and forcefully. It wasn't a religion; it was a spell that needed breaking, a delusion that people could only wake from if shaken violently.

After some months of this insanity, my husband (God bless him) announced that he was leaving the ministry whether I came or not. I was more attached to the place and the people than he, so this faced me with a hard decision. I had to choose between my marriage and the ministry. I chose my marriage (God bless me). The leader, however, urged me to stay behind. "Don't go back to Egypt," he said, "Stay here where God has led you."

"I love the witnessing opportunities and the fellowship, but I have to leave," I said.

He replied with a threat, "Your talents will go to waste if you leave, and you'll be abandoning God's call for your life." He knew just what buttons to push. I had, in fact, developed many gifts at the ministry and feared losing those opportunities.

"Michael is my husband. It's the right thing to do. I can't ignore my conscience," I protested.

"You can sear it!" he growled, implying that I was doing so by leaving.

This drove the nail in the coffin of my infatuation with the "works trip." This leader, who supposedly championed standards, whom I once thought embodied conservative Adventism, had enlisted me to sever a sacred relationship that no man should put asunder.

A rules-oriented religion always backfires eventually. Some have enough ego strength (or blind pride is a better term) to fool themselves that it's working. Jesus called them hypocrites. Most often, the pressure of a double life eventually causes emotional and even physical breakdown; this is one sense in which "the law worketh wrath" and "the letter kills" (Romans 4:15, KJV; 2 Corinthians 3:6).

Religionist beware—a Christless religion isn't just wrong, it's dangerous! This is why Seventh-day Adventists, with their complex and comprehensive list of admonitions, must forcefully and constantly preach the gospel of righteousness by faith. We must hold high the standard, at the same time repeatedly placing Jesus at dead center of all law and doctrine. The neglect of this has at times plagued our denomination and made it at times appear cult-like.

The brick wall was about to break for me, opening my field of vision to a more dazzling view of the gospel than I had thus far beheld.

"Brethren, shall we not all of us leave our loads there? And when we leave this meeting, may it be with the truth burning in our souls like fire shut up in our bones. You will meet with those who will say, 'You are too much excited over this matter. You are too much in earnest. You should not be reaching for the righteousness of Christ, and making so much of that. You should preach the law.' As a people, we have preached the law until we are as dry as the hills of Gilboa that had neither dew nor rain. We must preach Christ in the law, and there will be sap and nourishment in the preaching that will be as food to the famishing flock of God. We must not trust in our own merits at all, but in the merits of Jesus of Nazareth. Our eyes must be anointed with eye-salve. We must draw nigh to God, and he will draw nigh to us, if we come in his own appointed way. O that you may go forth as the disciples did after the day of Pentecost, and then your testimony will have a living ring, and souls will be converted to God."[4]

Endnotes

1) I'm not here for social reasons, primarily. I wasn't raised in the church, so I'm not an "institutional Adventist." I found Jesus before I knew what an Adventist was, and I believe He led me here. I also believe that the Christian message taken to its logical and Biblical conclusion in these end times results in Adventist teachings. I believe that the gospel established at the founding of the Christian faith, and reclaimed through the Reformation, finds its most complete expression in the message that lies at the heart of this denomination. Again, if I didn't believe that, I'd look elsewhere for a church. I wouldn't want to in any way influence people to embrace such a "heavy" message if it wasn't also true.

2) See, for instance, Jeremiah 28:9; John 16:13; 2 Peter 1:20, 21; Micah 3:5-8; Isaiah 24:20, 21; 1 Corinthians 13:2, 3; Isaiah 8:20; 1 John 4:1-3; Matthew 7:16-20; Deuteronomy 18:18.

3) For more on my recovery from eating disorders, read *Dying to be Beautiful*, Review and Herald Publishing.

4) *Advent Review and Sabbath Herald*, March 11, 1890.

Chapter Two
Law, Grace, Gospel

Not to dogmatize Biblical terms, but let me tell you how I define law, grace, and the gospel. Law is the expression of God's character, codified in His commandments. Grace is the outpouring of mercy, favor, and power to sinners, leading them to obey the commandments. The gospel is the proclamation of God's saving grace in the context of His law. The law is cruel without grace, and grace is pointless without the law. Although most of us are skewed toward one or the other, law and grace are in reality inseparable partners. You already know that as a young Christian, I was skewed toward the law (maybe since, I've become too grace-biased, but that topic is for another book).

My rules-based to gospel-based journey was a microcosm of the Adventist church's macrocosm. I think every spiritual unit—whether a person or ministry or the denomination itself—passes through a similar series of phases. First, standards and beliefs are seized and valued, but rigidly, as if in fear of losing them. Then bravado and denial are gradually tempered as the rubber hits the road and failure raises its ugly head. Finally, there is a recognition of human inadequacy; youthful overconfidence is eventually tempered, leading to a gentler, more sustainable religion.

The Adventist church was once young and overconfident. The pioneers mined the Word of God and were signally led to unearth several Bible truths. Ellen White began to manifest the gift of prophecy. Through her, God bequeathed to the church a bounty of admonitions, counsels, and encouragements. The call to evangelize activated the church further. The pioneers passionately devoted themselves to the cause of proclaiming the Sabbath and other truths. Because they so avidly studied the Bible, Adventists consistently won the well-attended religious debates of the day. The church grew exponentially. In spite of these triumphs, an insidious tragedy inserted itself into the narrative. As a result of early successes, the collective ego of Adventism began to swell, and slowly, imperceptibly, Jesus Christ was nudged out of the picture.

Ellen White was unhappy with this. Fortunately, God was already at work, preparing two young men to bring revival and change. Alonzo Jones and Ellet Waggoner were from two different worlds, but of one mind when they discovered the message of righteousness by faith. Jones was a converted army sergeant who had vowed to dedicate all to Christ. Waggoner had a more extraordinary conversion. A lifelong Adventist, he conformed to status quo until one day he experienced a kind of waking vision:

"I was sitting a little apart from the body of the congregation in the large tent at a camp meeting in Healdsburg [California], one gloomy Sabbath afternoon. I have no idea what was the subject of the discourse. Not a word nor a text have I ever known. All that has remained with me was what I saw. Suddenly a light shone round me, and the tent was for me far more brilliantly lighted than if the noon-day sun had been shining, and I saw Christ hanging on the cross, crucified for me. In that moment I had my first positive knowledge, which came like an overwhelming flood, that God loved me, and that Christ died for me. God and I were the only beings I was conscious of in the universe. I knew then, by actual sight, that God was in Christ reconciling the world unto Himself, and I was the whole world with all its sin. I am sure that Paul's experience on the way to Damascus was no more real than mine . . ."[1]

Jones and Waggoner met when called to co-edit a denominational magazine, Signs of the Times. They compared notes, shared their stories, and probed the Word of God for light, convinced that religion promised something more than they knew. The message that emerged accomplished something Protestantism hadn't—communicated Christ and His righteousness in the context of all ten commandments. Instead of delivering believers from obedience, their message led to obedience. One would think this would please the "old guard," who cherished the law, but like the Pharisees of Jesus' day they resisted the humbling message that human works have no merit before God. Thus the 1888 Message wasn't officially accepted. Fortunately, that didn't completely prevent its spread to the hungering, thirsting people. Thank God for grass roots!

My own transition from law to grace was similar.

Ministry life was exhilarating, and I rode high on the successes of it for many years. Along with friends and co-workers, I cherished a sense of privilege, having been blessed with present truth. As was true with early Adventism, a subtle spiritual pride seeped into my ideal little world. Fortunately, I began to receive little wake-up calls that something more was needed. One moment of truth came as I was writing a song for children entitled "Very Special Friend," with the following lyrics:

Do you know the truest Friend of all?
He is a very special Friend
He will love you even if you fall
That is why He is the truest Friend of all

I gasped as I read the words I had written. I was filled with doubt, imploring my own conscience, "He will love us even if we fall? If I say that, won't it give people license to sin?" But then I was equally shocked at my questioning of such a basic truth as God's unconditional love. I struggled to harmonize the call to obedience and the kindness of God.

Another flash of self-awareness came one day as I was riding home in a van full of people from a long day of work at the health ministry. It was Friday. Normally on Friday nights, we had a worship service in the big living room of a mansion that housed about twenty-five of the staff. This was the high point of the week. We would sing hymns until we were hoarse, then one by one share witnessing stories. Our sessions were punctuated with laughter and sometimes tears, filled with a kind of irrepressible excitement that I miss to this day.

When we finished the hour-plus session of sharing, someone, usually the director, would share a spiritual thought or two and then give a report of the worldwide mission field. We would hear of associate ministries being developed in faraway France, England, and even Austria, as well as all over the U.S. Awestruck, we felt to our depths that this ministry was on the cutting edge. We believed that God was using us mightily. In fact, we thought we were at the forefront of the finishing of the great commission. We had a grandiosity problem.

On this particular van ride, I remember asking who was speaking for worship that night. When one of the men volunteered that he had been chosen, I found myself blurting something out almost against my will. "Could you talk about the cross? We haven't heard about the cross in so long! Please talk about the cross!"

I realized that we had been like wedding guests who, caught up in the festivities, forgot who was getting married. It is truly remarkable how human beings can get so absorbed in religion that they forget God. But for me the constant rehearsal of man's works was beginning to take its toll, and I found myself yearning to hear about God's work.

About this time the director of the institution began to be exposed as a philanderer. As long-concealed confessions released themselves from burdened hearts, he seemed all the more inflamed. What ensued was a drama that more closely resembled a soap opera than a ministry. It wasn't long before he set his sights on me. Given his position of authority, I was extremely pressured to yield to his designs. I admit I was at times woefully giddy with the flattery of his attention. Thank God, the Holy Spirit finally succeeded in breaking the spell. I came forward with my story, after which several more stories tumbled out. The sinful cat was out of the religious façade-bag.

Leaving the ministry broke my heart and extruded my husband and me into a lonely world. I bore our first child soon after and was tethered to home life. As the quiet hours passed, I reflected, asking, "What next,

God?" Soon after, a friend approached us with some materials he'd been reading. He explained excitedly that he had begun studying the message of righteousness by faith. Social influence again bore sway, and my husband and I began to study the materials and compare notes with others. Gradually, blessedly, good news began to seep into the vacuum that works religion created. We learned that we weren't the first legalism-burned believers in the world, that in fact the very origins of our church featured a legalism-to-gospel narrative similar to ours. We also learned that Ellen White played a leading role in that drama, and that she embraced the gospel message delivered by Jones and Waggoner. Here are some of her hundreds of endorsements:

> "It bears divine credentials, and its fruit is unto holiness."[2]
> "Light and freedom and the outpouring of the Spirit of God have attended the work."[3]
> "[They are] Christ's delegated messengers."[4]

As we studied, we wondered, why did it take ten years in Adventism before we learned this message? History answered that question. We learned that 1888 is one of the most discussed and debated dates in Adventism. Jones and Waggoner were ostracized, even persecuted, for bearing it. "Spiritual bloodbath" isn't too strong a word to describe the attending fracas. The "old guard" and the "new guard" were at sword's point for years afterwards; if not for the mediations of Ellen White, there may have been an unsalvageable rift.

How silly, given that the message would only have supported our doctrinal platform. Because of the inheritance of truth bequeathed to Seventh-day Adventists, we are in the very best position to comprehend Christ, His mission, His sacrifice, and His high priestly ministry. The 1888 message was given to build upon this foundation and further flesh out our denominational portrait of Christ. So many students of the righteousness by faith message, including myself, fall in love with Jesus all over again.

This obscure conference, that for all appearances should have passed unmarked into the archives of Seventh-day Adventist history, still agitates us today. Many forums, sponsored by both leadership and laity, have since been organized to study and debate the issue. In light of all this I'd like to ask a simple question. Why can't we let it go?

Perhaps the answer to this "why?" is the same as the answer to others. Why did Ellen White sit on the front pew at the 1888 conference, face aglow, so thrilled that she later wrote, "Every fiber of my heart said amen"?[5] Why, in the years following, did she write a total of 1,821 pages of commentary regarding the message and its surrounding issues? Why did she say only a few years later that the message could have prepared the church and the world for the coming of Christ?

In short, what was so great about righteousness by faith?

"The Lord in His great mercy sent a most precious message to His people through Elders Waggoner and Jones. This message was to bring more prominently before the world the uplifted Savior, the sacrifice for the sins of the whole world. It presented justification through faith in the Surety; it invited the people to receive the righteousness of Christ, which is made manifest in obedience to all the commandments of God. Many had lost sight of Jesus. They needed to have their eyes directed to His divine person, His merits, and His changeless love for the human family. All power is given into His hands, that He may dispense rich gifts unto men, imparting the priceless gift of His own righteousness to the helpless human agent. This is the message that God commanded to be given to the world. It is the third angel's message, which is to be proclaimed with a loud voice, and attended with the outpouring of His Spirit in a large measure."[6]

Endnotes

1) Letter, May 16, 1916.

2) *Review and Herald*, March 5, 1884.

3) Letter, January 9, 1893.

4) *Testimonies to Ministers*, pp. 96, 97.

5) *The Ellen White 1888 Materials*, pp. 349.

6) *Ibid*, page 1336, 1337.

Chapter Three
The Delay

Adventism has its own language. One of our most tossed-about terms is "the third angel's message." This alludes to the passage found in Revelation 14:6-13, which depicts three angels shouting God's final warning to earth. The third angel warns of the "mark of the beast" so often speculated on in Christian circles. Let me say up front that I believe the Adventist church's teaching on the identity of the beast. It fully harmonizes with the Bible. I also believe that in these last days, the third angel's message is central, pivotal, essential, and indispensable.

So, what is the mark of the beast? Is it the issuing of the Social Security number, as some believed in 1930? Or is it the Internet, and Bill Gates the antichrist? Is it a credit card, or a computer chip? Speculative theories abound. If we let the Bible speak, though, there's no need to speculate. We see that the mark is spiritual/religious in nature, an indicator of allegiance to Babylon (apostate religious powers), to the beast (a religio-political collusion), and ultimately to Satan himself. Here it is in distilled form: The mark of the beast is a religious observance kept in obedience to state-sponsored, apostate Christianity in the end times. Adventists believe that there will come a time when Sunday observance will be mandated by the church-state. Then, Sunday observance will be the mark of the beast. But that's not my main point . . .

The message of the third angel is heaven's red-alert against this insidious mark. As earth's history winds down, the world divides into the Lamb's camp and the beast's camp. The followers of Jesus are disallowed from buying and selling (Revelation 13:17) and hunted like animals (Revelation 13:15) by the beast-camp. It's a horrific scene of globalized politics gone bad. The ever-warring powers of the world have finally joined under one wicked banner and have turned their guns on an obscure band of Christians. The third angel says these persecutors will be "tormented with fire and brimstone," and that the saints who withstand them "keep the commandments of God and the faith of Jesus," (Revelation 14:10, 12).

Think about it. Something powerful must sustain the believers to stand firm in the face of starvation and death. Revelation reveals that something to be the gospel, called the third angel's message because it will essentially "fly" through its communicators to every inhabitant of the world. The gospel message in the context of all ten commandments produces a synergy that blazes forth with such power that it melts hearts of the willing and hardens the unwilling like a pottery kiln. The third angel's message is the essential oil of the gospel, extracted through the ages and presented in richness to the final generation of earth. Its nourishment is needed to sustain believers through the most subtle and insidious spiritual/moral test of all time. And, according to Ellen White, God gave this message through Jones and Waggoner in 1888.

With this in mind, read what Ellen White said about it in 1893:

"The influence that grew out of the resistance of light and truth at Minneapolis, tended to make of no effect the light God had given to his people. . . If every soldier of Christ had done his duty, if every watchman on the walls of Zion had given the trumpet a certain sound, the world might ere this have heard the message of warning. But the work is years behind. What account will be rendered to God for thus retarding the work?"[1]

The essence of this statement is devastating. It was written in 1893. The world might have been warned and Jesus might have come by 1893 if our brethren had embraced righteousness by faith! This presents a plethora of spiritual issues.

For instance, think about the responsibility, even guilt, implied. Since 1893 we have seen World War I, World War II, Lenin, Stalin, the Holocaust; the Korean War, Vietnam, Cambodia, Kuwait, Bosnia,

Sudan, Iraq, etc. Each one of these atrocities led to the death of millions, many of whom entered their graves unsaved. Smaller wars have abounded. Disasters such as the San Francisco Earthquake and the Great Chicago Fire claimed thousands. Chernobyl's radiation still eats away at the innocent. The Great Irish Famine, Typhoid Mary, AIDS—the list is unending. These tragedies are but identifiable markers on the greater sea of all human suffering. Every rape, murder, and abuse, every suicide, every broken heart, every mental illness, abandoned child, battered wife, and lonely old man—preventable. Time has ground on, churning out victims of circumstance like so many condemned prisoners numbly marching in the cold. All in the last century. All because of the delay. Wow!

Ideas like these cause quite a stir. Some say that God has a scheduled time for Christ's return. Others cite free will, claiming that the coming of Jesus is in our hands. The Bible seems to support both a divine timetable and human influence on the time of Christ's return. Essentially, this paradox involves divine sovereignty versus human free will. It is difficult to understand how these two things can coexist.

A return to Jesus' first coming will help. In Acts 2:23, we read that Jesus was "delivered up by the predetermined plan and foreknowledge of God." In other words, God planned Jesus' death. In the next breath, Peter tells the Jews, "You nailed [Him] to a cross by the hands of godless men, and put Him to death." Crunch these two facts together, and you have something like, "God willed it, but humans did it." I summarize the matter this way: God knew what man would do with His Son. Pure love would evoke pure hate from carnal humanity. Jesus would end up on a cross. God didn't have to pull any puppet strings or program any robots to conjure up this reaction. It was volitional. Yet it was His privilege as Cosmic Sovereign to mold the raw materials produced by human choice into something He could use for His own purposes. God took the ashes of sin and molded from them the beauty of salvation. He took the most egregious sin of human history and fashioned from it the best Gift that the Godhead could give. God took the crucifixion and shaped it into the Cross. He redeemed our failure, ultimately using our failure to redeem us.

Applying this principle to the tragedy of Jesus' delay, we can know that God will redeem it as well. After all, we owe our existence to the lingering of time. More importantly, millions more will be saved eternally because of the delay. There is forgiveness. There is redemption. I'm not saying that we should bear the weight of the sin of one hundred and fifty years and counting. What I am saying is that we should now do all we can to hasten the coming of Jesus.

Far from betraying some uncomely weakness in God, a waiting Christ tells us of God's compassion, clearly seen in 2 Peter 3:9: "The Lord is not slow about His promise, as some count slowness, but is patient toward you, not wishing for any to perish but for all to come to repentance." What does God wish to avoid? That "any should perish." What does He wait for? "For all to come to repentance." What is the logical conclusion? That "God's unwillingness to have His people perish has been the reason for the so long delay."[2] My friends, God is waiting for believers to believe.

Here are some basic facts about Jesus' coming which have helped guide my understanding:

1. *The gospel will be preached globally*. Jesus placed time's cutoff point just after the gospel has been "preached in the whole world" (Matthew 24:14). The finishing of the gospel commission depends upon the cooperation of human beings, namely, His church.

2. *The harvest will ripen*. The prepared world is described in prophecy as a "ripe harvest," of which Jesus is told to "put in [His] sickle and reap" (Revelation 14:15). The harvest principle is also found in the parable of the tares: "allow both [the wheat and the tares] to grow together until the harvest" (Matthew 13:30). This parable applies to the end of the world, when "there will be no likeness between good and evil. Then those who have joined the church, but who have not joined Christ,

will be manifest."[4] In other words, character will ripen, and the end will come.

3. *Christ's character will be manifested.* "When the character of Christ shall be perfectly reproduced in His people, then He will come to claim them as His own."[5] Jesus waits for the manifestation of Himself in His professed followers. He will not return to receive strangers, but familiar friends. The earth will be separated into two groups—those who know Him, and those who know Him not. Those who know Him will "see Him as He is" (see 1 John 3:2), but those who know Him not will be destroyed by that same brightness, for "the glory of Him who is love will destroy them."[6] Jesus delays His coming because He knows that His love is a consuming fire to the sin-tainted heart. Only when He is sure that sinners are intractable will He venture to unveil His glorious Self. To come before that time would be to destroy what could have been saved.

4. *The sanctuary will be cleansed.* Adventism's most solemn and unique teaching is the doctrine of the cleansing of the heavenly sanctuary. It teaches that Christ is now in heaven as High Priest, engaging in the process of eradicating sin, just as Israel's high priest cleansed the sanctuary during Yom Kippur (Leviticus 16). You see, God is faced with two great objectives—to destroy sin and to save sinners. The cleansing of the heavenly sanctuary teaches us how these will take place—through the painstaking, compassionate ministration of Jesus in heaven. Through His prayers to God and pleadings to us, sin is blotted out or retained on our life record. This process will precede the harvest, and according to Ellen White's statement in 1893, it would have been greatly catalyzed by the third angel's message.

So, what is the heart of that message? Consider this: "Several have written to me, inquiring if the message of justification by faith is the third angel's message, and I have answered, 'It is the third angel's message in verity.'" [10] This statement was written in 1890, only two years after the conference when that message was first presented. The evidence is clear—

righteousness by faith is, "in verity," the heart of the third angel's message. And in 1888, we lost our heart.

Has it been found? That question burns. It is true that the church on the whole has grown out of its early legalism into a more gospel-based approach. But a greater reception and proclamation are yet to come. Otherwise, why the tedious droning on of years, now more than a century of them, since the time when Jesus could have come?

When I first heard the 1888 message, I had that "this is it" feeling—the same feeling that came when I learned of Adventism itself. First I found the body of evidence, and now found the heart of the body. It's my desire to share within the context of my own fumbling Christian experience something of this heart.

Endnotes

1) *General Conference Daily Bulletin*, Feb. 28, 1893.

2) *Testimonies, vol. 2*, pp. 192, 194.

3) *Education*, p. 263; "The cross is a revelation to our dull senses of the pain that, from its very inception, sin has brought to the heart of God. Every departure from the right, every deed of cruelty, every failure of humanity to reach His ideal, brings grief to Him."

4) *Christ's Object Lessons*, p. 74.

5) *Ibid.*, p. 69.

6) *Desire of Ages*, p.764.

7) *Acts of the Apostles*, p. 12.

8) *The Great Controversy*, p. 607.

9) *Life Sketches*, pp. 95, 96; "I was shown that the third angel proclaiming the commandments of God and the faith of Jesus, represents the people who receive this message, and raise the voice of warning to the world to keep the commandments of God and His law as the apple of the eye; and that in response to this warning, many would embrace the Sabbath of the Lord."

10) *1st Selected Messages*, p. 372.

Chapter Four
A Savior Near

It was the fall of 1989. My husband and I had left the health ministry in New York when we discovered I was pregnant with baby number one. Shortly after she was born, we rented a small solar house in the middle of a huge dandelion field in southern Massachusetts, where a little sister was born. We were so blessed to have two healthy children, an intact family, and food on the table, youth, strength, love, and God's sweet presence in our home.

But there were problems. At thirty-one I developed allergies. Not just allergies to a few foods, but to every food. Not just to pollen in the spring, but to everything that suspended itself in the air, from mold spores to dust-mite feces. I was tired and lethargic, and worst of all, my entire respiratory tract swelled.

This wouldn't be a big deal for most, but I was a singer. Slowly it dawned upon me that my pipes were suffering. The tone wasn't as clear, the pitch wasn't as perfect, and the volume wasn't as strong. I fell prey to frequent, debilitating respiratory infections. Songs still played inside of me, but the more I tried to coordinate my swollen vocal chords, the more frustrated I became. My songwriting and singing had been my "contribution" and a source of self-worth, and now I was losing my career, my health, and my ministry in one package, or so I thought. I started to panic.

Medical help was my next resort. One doctor thought sinus surgery might be the answer, so I had one, then two, and in the end four sinus surgeries. When these didn't help, I became a favorite of every multi-level marketing supplement salesperson who descended upon me like bees on a watermelon slice. The blue-green, fiber-filled, enzyme-rich, phyto-blast concoctions, without exception, came guaranteed to cure me, and without exception didn't. I tried strict diets and elimination diets, mono diets, fasting, hydrotherapy, and massage. And of course I tried prayer, but nothing helped. Nothing.

When the realization that my condition was chronic hit me, it felt like a coffin had been nailed shut over my still-living body. *Why me?* I demanded of God when I could bring myself to speak to Him. I took walks in the forest and fields while my children were napping and begged Him to give me a reason for my misfortune. My worst fears took over; not only did I exaggerate the damage, but I spiritualized it, thinking God was punishing or rejecting me. As despairing thoughts tumbled in on one another, the heavens stared back as silent as stone. Once that feeling settled (it's called clinical depression), it was as hard to shake as a bloodsucker. Oh, I carried on—functioned because I had to, loved my children because they needed it, smiled because the world was a sad place, but I was plagued inside. Worst of all, religion didn't seem to help. Phrases like "trust God" lost their meaning, and church started to feel like a foreign country.

Depression is when all the worst dreads that you house in your unconscious come flying up like bats out of hell. You don't see anything but the chaos of your own negativity, and you don't trust anyone to help you, even though you are helpless to fight it alone. Normal depression is brought on by circumstances, but in susceptible people a short-term bout can lead into chronic depression. This was me.

I realize now that great difficulty is God's way of saying, "My grace is sufficient." My goody-goody religion was far too brittle to survive a major life crisis, but thank God, when it shattered into a thousand pieces there was a saving message to fall back on. "God is faithful, who will not allow you to be tempted beyond what you are able, but with the temptation will also make the way of escape, that you may be able to bear it" (1 Corinthians 10:13, NKJV). He allowed the "message of His healing grace"[1] to come into my life when the healing was the most desperately needed.

When someone is ill or discouraged, the typical human response is to avoid him or her. If you aren't convinced of this, become ill or discouraged, and then count your friends. You may need only one finger—for Jesus. This is basically the situation in which I found myself. There were a few souls brave enough to meet me in my dark valley, but it was usually to blurt out a few platitudes, pray as if they were warding off evil spirits, and then flee. As never before, I sensed how incapable most humans are of entering into the pain of another. Thankfully, the loneliness of this realization only made the truths I was learning more welcome.

As I studied, I realized that God's response to human suffering was the opposite of the typical human response. In short, God drew near at the point where people drew back. One of the most prominent thoughts in all of Jones and Waggoner's teaching was the nearness of the Savior. As Jones put it, Jesus "has come to us just where we are." He prefaces this thought with:

"The idea of the natural mind [is] that God is too pure and too holy to dwell with us and in us in our sinful human nature; that sinful as we are, we are too far off for Him in His purity and holiness to come to us just where we are."[2]

A detached, distant Savior could not have helped me out of my depression. A Savior near was what I needed.

The nature of Christ has been hotly debated among Adventists, featuring two theological camps: "prelapsarian" and "postlapsarian." Prelapsarians believe that Jesus had the nature of Adam before the Fall (*pre*-lapse), and postlapsarians believe He had the nature of Adam after the Fall (*post*-lapse). Historically, Adventism favored the postlapsarian position, but in the 1950s Protestant leaders began to frame this as cult-like and contrary to orthodox Christianity. In the 1950s some high-level Adventist leadership responded with a book called *Questions on Doctrine*. This altering of our position created an outcry within the church which still reverberates today in some circles.

Theology can be difficult. Doctrines are crisp and clear, fact-based and provable. In contrast, theology is a "softer" science, more fluid and subject to the inconsistencies of expression and the limitations of words. Deep spiritual truths, such as the nature of Christ, require a certain negotiation between two seemingly contradictory poles of truth. This Biblical balancing is different than philosophical dialectics, which "balance" thesis (a theory) and antithesis (a contrasting theory) to form a synthesis (combination). This practice blends truth and error to make more error. In contrast, Biblical thinking balances two *truths* that, on the surface, seem to oppose one another to arrive at their deep, underlying harmony. In contrast to normal rational process, a comprehension of truth requires our human faculties plus the divine illumination of the Holy Spirit.

While I couldn't claim to be unbiased, I saw value in statements on both ends of the nature of Christ spectrum. Did He have a prelapsasrian or postlapsarian nature? I didn't feel it necessary to choose. He was an entirely new order of human being—divine perfection housed in sinful flesh. We were innately sinful, while He was innately sinless. A Spirit-led interpretation respects the tension between Jesus' sinlessness and His sharing of our fallen condition. Some examples of the former are:

"We should have no misgivings in regard to the perfect sinlessness of the human nature of Christ."[3]

"For such an high priest became us, who is holy, harmless, undefiled, separate from sinners" (Hebrews 7:26, NKJV).

And the latter:

"In Him was no guile or sinfulness; He was ever pure and undefiled; yet He took upon Him our sinful nature."[4]

"For four thousand years the race had been decreasing in physical strength, in mental power, and in moral worth; and Christ took upon Him the infirmities of degenerate humanity."[5]

"Wherefore in all things it behooved him to be made like unto his brethren... For in that He himself hath suffered being tempted, he is able to succour them that are tempted" (Hebrews 2:17, 18, KJV).

These statements seemed to contradict one another until I noticed something in the "postlapsarian" verses. Never did inspiration indicate that Jesus "had" a sinful nature, but that He "took" our sinful nature, or was "made" like us:

> "*Made* to be sin for us" (1 Corinthians 5:21)
> "*Made* in the likeness of men" (Philippians 2:7)
> "*Took* part of the same" (Hebrews 2:14)
> "*Made* like unto his brethren" (Hebrews 2:17)
> "He *assumed* the liabilities of human nature."[6]
> "He *took* upon His sinless nature our sinful nature."[7]
> "Our Savior *took* humanity, with all its liabilities."[8]

This was the key to understanding how Jesus could be innately sinless, yet bear our sin so personally that He could empathize completely. He was *made* into, *assumed* and *took* what was not His by native right. He "had" a sinless nature, but "took" our sinful nature. Significantly, the bearing of our sinful nature in the incarnation was the first step toward the bearing of the full weight of our sin at the cross. The incarnation was therefore the first manifestation of the love that would ultimately drive Jesus to yield up His life on Calvary. He was *made* in the likeness of men, *made* like unto His brethren, and would be "made a curse for us" (Galatians 3:13).

Adventist brethren wrestled with this during the 1888 era. Some felt that for Jesus to assume fallen nature would make him into a sinner. The subtleties of these arguments may be beyond the scope of this book and even beyond my ken as a thinker, but the logic that Waggoner presented really makes sense to me. He said:

"You are shocked at the idea that Jesus was born under the condemnation of the law, because he never committed a sin in his life. But you admit that on the cross he was under the condemnation of the law. What! Had he then committed sin? Not by any means. Well, then, if Jesus could be under the condemnation of the law at one time in his life, and be sinless, I see no reason why he could not be under the condemnation of the law at another time, and still be sinless."⁹ A little confession here; I feel inadequate to tackle this issue, and fearful of placing myself on one side of an ongoing debate I don't really want to partake in. But I had to risk these things in order to say what I really want to say, which is: Jesus became one of us. Speaking for myself on this point, the awareness that the Son of God stepped into the midst of fallen humanity was powerful medicine for my soul as I fought to recover from depression. In Jesus I saw a Savior who knew just how I felt. When I prayed to Him, I saw compassionate eyes rather than the blank stare of a foreigner who couldn't decode my language. "For we do not have a high priest who cannot sympathize with our weaknesses, but One who has been tempted in all things as we are, yet without sin" (Hebrews 4:15). We "do not" have a high priest who "cannot" sympathize is a double negative meaning that we *do* have a high priest who *can* sympathize. As the great hymn *Oh, Holy Night* says, "He knows our needs, to our weakness He's no stranger." I agree. Sinless Jesus is no Stranger to our weaknesses! He feels them to His core, "yet without sin." Let's not let the paradox of those two things keep us from appreciating them both.

Whatever doubts you may have about human therapists, empirical studies show that counseling *works*. Researchers spend thousands of dollars and hours of time to identify the effective aspect of counseling. A survey of the data reveals that it all boils down to the empathy of the therapist. Empathy is medicine. If empathy from fickle, selfish, short-sighted sinners "works," how much more the selfless empathy of Jesus? We are human and must look into a human face for comfort. God has a human face now, and His name is Jesus.

I was grateful to be reminded that Jesus knew the blinding sorrow I was experiencing. Every one of us has a personal dark place that no human loved one or friend can enter. Jesus will meet us there. Time and time again I have experienced this as my synapses have activated the old thought patterns of despair. Time and time again the dark, lonely places of my life are sweetened by the presence of Jesus. Almost to the point—yes, to the point—where I thank God for the darkness.

Laden with their own weaknesses and temptations, Jones and Waggoner brought before people a Savior who was near rather than afar off. A century and a half later the ripple effect of their message came to my shore and reminded me that, "Our griefs He Himself bore, and our sorrows He carried" (Isaiah 53:4).

Endnotes

1) *The Ellen G. White 1888 Materials*, p. 409.

2) Jones, A. T., *The Consecrated Way*, p. 31.

3) *Signs of the Times,* June 9, 1898.

4) *Review and Herald,* Dec. 15, 1896.

5) *Desire of Ages,* p. 117.

6) *Signs of the Times,* Aug. 2, 1905.

7) *Medical Ministry,* p. 181.

8) *The Desire of Ages,* p. 117.

9) E. J. Waggoner, *The Gospel in Galatians*, pp. 62, 63, Feb. 19, 1887.

Chapter Five
His Gifts to the World

Christians often give short shrift to what is called the "universal effect of the cross." We hesitantly admit that Jesus' sacrifice was for all the world, but quickly follow with multiple qualifications. We say things like, "If we don't accept it, it will do us *no good!*" making it sound as if the cross has had no effect where it is not understood, appreciated, and received.

Yet every blessing that flows from God does so through the conduit of Calvary. When we fail to adequately establish what the cross did for every person, we deprive ourselves and others of the substance toward which faith is exercised. The net result of this is faith in faith—a self-defeating proposition. Because true faith rests upon God's work and not our own, I'll spend this chapter establishing what His cross accomplished for every man, woman, and child. "When we were yet without strength, in due time Christ died for the ungodly" (Romans 5:6). God has given us all a rich inheritance in Jesus. These gifts are truth-statements, or *declaratives* of the gospel. God's requirements, or *imperatives,* come later, after His great initiative in the plan of salvation has been established. In the circles I once ran in, there was a strong focus on imperatives and little focus on declaratives. This was because the imperatives involved human effort, and we liked that topic. Overcoming sin was of great importance to us. We might give brief lip service to some of the great themes of the atonement, but they were quickly followed by "But . . . " *But if we don't accept, but if we don't obey, but if we don't change, but, but, but.* We couldn't just state the facts of God's free gifts and let them hang in the air. This was a problem! Emphasizing human effort without a preparatory emphasis on God's free gift of salvation is like requiring a child to love and obey a distant-but-demanding father. We engage in a kind of sacrilegious role-reversal when we enlist human response without adequately establishing the initiatives of God. But it's not too late. Let's declare the declaratives now and just let them soak into our wounded consciousness. What did God do in Christ before humanity so much as lifted a finger in response? What are some of His gifts to the world?

Salvation. After years of being marginalized by the Jews, the Samaritans joyfully identified Jesus as the "*Savior of the world*" (John 4:42). Spiritual Jews of today do great harm when they overly narrow God's salvation to a chosen few. He "desires all men to be saved" and is "not wishing that any should perish" (1 Timothy 2:4; 2 Peter 3:9).

But isn't it true that eternal salvation is on condition of faith? Yes, but remember that before Jesus could save any individual, He had to save humanity. Jesus is called the "Savior of all men, *especially of those who believe*" (1 Timothy 4:10, NKJV, italics supplied). In this verse we see a two-phase process—a universal phase in which salvation is *supplied* to all, and a personal phase in which it is *applied* to believers. This is the progression we see in all aspects of God's salvation; He first bestows the gift—salvation, justification, redemption, reconciliation—then enlists acceptance of the gift.

Understanding and recounting God's free gifts to the world helps even committed Christians find their way back to God when they've strayed. Why? Because there's a lost soul in every one of us who is tempted to believe that God really doesn't care whether we live or die. When we see Jesus as "the lamb slain from the foundation of the world" (Revelation 13:8), and remember that the fires of hell were not designed for any human being, but rather for "the devil and his angels" (Matthew 25:41), our insecurities are calmed and we feel safe to return to Him. More than this, we are like the prisoner who learns that war is over—impelled by the revelation of good news to run, shouting, through the streets. In fact, gospel-born confidence always spills out in evangelism.

Justification. The Bible uses several metaphors to convey all that salvation entails. Every metaphor is good and necessary, but none is complete or superior. One of the most prevalent is the legal metaphor, or justification, which is woven throughout the Old Testament,[1] the teachings of Jesus[2] and of course, the writings of Paul. The teaching can be boiled down into a simple forensic formula: We sinned, God condemns sin, Jesus bore our condemnation, we exercise faith in His sacrifice, and we are free from condemnation, or "justified." The modern theological term for this is "substitution."

It's important to distinguish Biblical substitution from pagan substitution. The latter depicts an angry deity venting his pent-up rage on an innocent, but unrelated, victim. This led to human sacrifice in ancient times[3] and will lead to similar atrocities in the future.[4] In the Christianized version of this, Jesus is God's whipping boy, the unwitting recipient of God's rage-lust. Contrast this with the Biblical picture that "God was in Christ," and "the counsel of peace shall be between them both" (2 Corinthians 5:19; Zechariah 6:13, KJV). The agony of the Cross throbbed through the entire Godhead; it was a collaborative event with each member playing their respective roles; "God Himself was crucified with Christ; for Christ was one with the Father."[5] This "connectedness" extends to the human race. Not only was Jesus united to God, but to humanity as well, a divine-human bridge over the black chasm hewn by sin. Jesus was made "in the likeness of sinful flesh and for sin" and so "condemned sin in the flesh," (Romans 8:3). He "shared in the same" flesh and blood so that "through death He might destroy him who had the power of death, that is, the devil, and release those who through fear of death were all their lifetime subject to bondage" (Hebrews 2:14, 15, NKJV). By assuming our fallen nature, Jesus was fitted up to become our perfect Representative. On that basis, He could be our perfect Substitute. This is one reason Christ's human nature is "everything to us."[6]

Substitution is sometimes expressed in the word "propitiation":

"Being justified freely by His grace through the redemption that is in Christ Jesus; whom God set forth as a *propitiation* in His blood" (Romans 3:24, 25, italics supplied). "Propitiation" is from the Greek *hilasterion,* which means "mercy seat"—the gold-plate covering on the ark in the most holy place of the sanctuary. This is the place where law and forgiveness harmonize. The ark contained the Ten Commandments. Above it blazed the Shekinah, the fiery presence of God. Once a year, the high priest atoned for the sins of Israel by sprinkling the blood of atonement on the mercy seat. The priest, representing the people, was not condemned by the law or consumed by the Shekinah glory because of that blood. In the same way, we sinners are spared condemnation because of the blood of our Substitute.

For whom is He a substitute? Jesus was the propitiation "for our sin; and not for ours only, but also for those of the *whole world*" (1 John 2:2, italics supplied). He bore the legal penalty of transgression for every man, woman, and child who ever lived and ever will live! Romans 5:18 says the cross resulted in "justification of life to all men." Isaiah predicted that God's "righteous Servant" would "justify the many, as He will bear their iniquities," (Isaiah 53:11). Jesus has absorbed the full weight of our punishment. Wrath has been expended and justice satisfied for every person. If it were not so, we wouldn't be enjoying this moment of contemplation.

Redemption. Moving from the courtroom to the marketplace, we embrace the commercial metaphor of redemption or "buying back." "Ransom" may be an even more accurate term,[7] and certainly evokes powerful images of a kidnapped child and a large payoff from a solicitous loved one. The instances of this metaphor are many: "The Son of Man did not come to be served, but to serve, and to give his life as a *ransom* for many" (Mark 10:45). "Christ Jesus . . . gave Himself as a *ransom* for all, the testimony borne at the proper time" (1 Timothy 2:5, 6). "In Him we have *redemption* through His blood, the forgiveness of our trespasses"

(Ephesians 1:7). "In whom we have *redemption*, the forgiveness of sins" (Colossians 1:14, all emphases mine).

To whom is the ransom paid? The answer to this question distinguishes Biblical ransom from the kind we read about in the newspapers. Not from a lurking, corrupt criminal were we bought back, but from the righteous consequences of God's law: "Christ redeemed us from the *curse of the law*, having become a curse for us" (Galatians 3:13, italics supplied). Jesus was "born under the law . . . in order that He might redeem those who were under the law" (Galatians 4:4, 5). Jesus came to us where we were held captive, and then through His death and resurrection carried us through the dark tunnel of the curse to new life. Because He had lived a sinless life, the grave had no right to hold Him. Jesus said, "'the ruler of this world is coming, and *he has nothing in Me*'" (John 14:30, italics supplied), and "'I lay down My life that I may take it again'" (John 10:17). We were captive, or "kidnapped" by the grave, but when Jesus "ascended on high, He led captivity captive," (Ephesians 4:8, NKJV). Now we are captive to the hope of everlasting life.

Reconciliation. The court of law and the marketplace are relatively cold places of rather formal transactions. This is why the relational aspect of the gospel is so needed, so heartwarming. God isn't just our Attorney or our Proprietor, He's the Heart of our hearts, our most intimate relation.

In any broken relationship, one party must initiate the process of healing. All world religions except Christianity feature the sinner seeking to bridge the gap with the divine through good works. Only the Christian gospel presents a God in search of humanity. Reconciliation evokes images of a Father calling into the howling wind in search of a runaway child. Such was our God when we strayed. But reconciliation demanded more than a simple rescue. Sin's alienation worked both ways; humanity was alienated from God, yes, but God was also alienated from humanity.[8] Before you conclude that this makes God seem less loving, remember that He resolved His own alienation problem by sending Jesus. The Cross, which is called "the reconciliation" (Romans 5:11), reopened the relationship between a holy God and His sinful children. This reconciliation took place "while we were enemies" (Romans 5:10). Don't miss this point! God didn't wait until we asked before He took the first step in repairing a broken bond. Salvation, justification, redemption, reconciliation—these are God's gifts to the world in Jesus. And the list goes on. Prior to studying the 1888 message, my focus had been on the dos and don'ts, but now they shifted to the hows and whys. A focus on the imperatives apart from the declaratives had created an insidious culture of will-worship. Now I began to realize why the Ten Commandments were preceded by God's declaration that He had delivered Israel, and why Paul's admonitions always followed eloquent grace-filled expositions. My new focus on gospel declaratives made, and still make, my heart leap with joy.

True obedience is a response to love. This is God's method, His mission and His character. He is the devoted Father who toiled for His children before ever asking them to obey. He took the first giant leap in sending Jesus, and we take our little baby steps in response to that unshakable historic fact. Imagine God's boldness! He sent Jesus without asking, without first sending a consent form or phoning us for an authorization. He "redeemed Adam's disgraceful fall, and saved the world"[9] whether we liked it or not.

Endnotes

1) The entire sanctuary service of the Old Testament was a legal procedure given under a theocracy.

2) See Luke 18:14.

3) *Desire of Ages,* p. 540: "Among the heathen, the dim consciousness that one was to die for the human race had led to the offering of human sacrifices."

4) Notice the death decree of Revelation 13:15. The beast, who institutes the death

decree, is a religious power.

5) *The Faith I Live By,* p. 50.

6) *Selected Messages One,* p. 243.

7) The words most often translated "redemption" and "redeem" are *lytroo* and *apolytrosis.* The root word of both is *lytron,* which means "price of release."

8) How is God reconciled to man?--By the work and merit of Jesus Christ, who has removed every objection, and put aside everything that would interpose between man and God's pardoning love," *Youth's Instructor,* Nov. 29, 1894.

9) *My Life Today,* p. 323.

Chapter Six
It's Time for a Funeral

I was at the local supercenter waiting for a prescription, and spotted a lady from church named Deloris. Bored with waiting, I remembered a little account I had to settle with this lady, who had often spoken out on controversial matters during Bible studies. Her comments were basically insinuations that the church was in apostasy. She had all the markings of what we might call a separatist, and seemed to think herself better informed and more obedient than others. I decided to walk over and pick a playful little fight with her. The ensuing discussion quickly became loud enough to make small waves in the generic-brand apple juice on a nearby shelf. I was quiet and composed (of course), but Deloris was a firm believer in the adage: "If you're losing an argument, simply raise the volume."

"Deloris, can't you see the difference between the church being in apostasy, and apostasy in the church?" I pled.

"Yes, but I think we've crossed the line," she said, "Women dress in immodest, worldly fashions!"

"That's true sometimes," I acquiesced.

"And the Seventh-day Adventist Church is *supposed* to be using natural remedies instead of drugs. But our hospitals give out drugs like candy!" she cried.

"True, preventative medicine, not acute care, was our calling as a church," I agreed, desperately hoping she wouldn't figure out it was "drugs" that brought me to the store in the first place.

"And the *music*!" she cried, "Rock and roll has no place in the church! It's worldly music!"

"So essentially, Deloris, you're saying that the church has a problem with sex, drugs, and rock-and-roll," I said.

"Yes!" she threw up her arms, nearly toppling the Maybelline Ultra-Lash stand.

Deloris's zeal for righteousness was exemplary, but she wasn't a great listener. She didn't really hear her opponent, but rather used the few seconds she allowed them to speak as time to form her next argument. Soon we had to agree to disagree and go our separate ways.

Don't you hate it when you think of the perfect thing to say *later*? As I walked to my car, I had my epiphany. Put this statement on an index card and tape it to your refrigerator:

Self-righteousness is just as seductive as sex, just as intoxicating as drugs, and just as rebellious as rock-and-roll.

In other words, we don't really need the sins of the flesh to be really good sinners—all we need is self-righteousness and we're rockin'. Self-righteousness is the mother lode, the aorta of sin. Out of its polluted streams flows the stinking manifestation of our inward decay. What if some Pharisees retain control of the outward expressions of sin? They are no better than hardened pustules—all the more toxic for the retention of their pus.

But then, maybe you're a pagan thinking, "Self-righteousness isn't my problem. I know I'm a sinner and I love my sins of the flesh. But at least I don't condemn other people's sins." Many hedonists take pride in their tolerance, but this doesn't prove what they want it to prove. It simply shows that they're just as self-righteous as their religious counterparts because they consider themselves superior in tolerance. It's true that the publican, and not the Pharisee, was justified, but why? Because the Pharisee said, "Thank God I'm not like other people"[1] His superior attitude blocked the reception of God's forgiveness. Whether we're superior about our religiosity or our heathenism, it's still the same core problem of self-righteousness. And self-righteousness will send us to hell.

What's the cure for this pervasive pandemic? This question frames the next logical step in the process of communicating the third angel's message. We've examined the Biblical evidence that in Christ God has given to every person a storehouse of gifts such as salvation, justification, redemption, and reconciliation. But while these temporarily stayed the consequences of sin, and provided for the human family a probationary life, salvation must be personally received in order to save us *eternally*. This personal reception is what we call "conversion," spoken of by Jesus as being "born again." Through receiving Jesus, the manifold gifts of God are imported into our personal experience, working a radical change; we are *individually* saved from sin, justified from its condemnation, redeemed from its captivity and reconciled to God.

The decision to die to self and be born again, to trade our own filthy rags for Jesus' spotless robe, is the most important decision we will ever make. Our future literally hangs upon it. Jesus first preached the "born-again" idea to Nicodemus, a Pharisee tempted to rest secure in his law-keeping. Many modern-day Nicodemuses have never been born again, renouncing their own righteousness and receiving Christ's. This is why the most Biblically correct denomination, the Seventh-day Adventist Church, needed a special presentation of the righteousness by faith message. With all our astute law-keeping and doctrinal exactitude, we were in danger of losing the forest of true Christianity for the trees of Adventist teaching.

Justification by faith is the lifeblood of the Bible, woven like a vascular system from the Creation story to the climax of John's vision. Paul was the great champion of the righteousness of Christ and its clearest, most comprehensive expositor. Here is one of his most salient statements, taken from Romans 3:21-24:

"But now apart from the law the righteousness of God has been manifested, being witnessed by the law and the prophets, even the righteousness of God through faith in Jesus Christ for all those who believe. For there is no distinction; for all have sinned and fall short of the glory of God, being justified as a gift by His grace through the redemption which is in Christ Jesus." A bullet-point distillation of these words is:

- There is righteousness available.
- We can't get it from the law.
- It's in Jesus.
- It comes to us "through faith."
- When we receive it, we are justified.
- Isn't that simple?
- God is an equal-opportunity justifier.

All have been given a measure of faith (Romans 12:3) and through it access to Jesus' righteousness. The Jews thought their law-keeping gave them access, and spiritual Jews are in danger of thinking the same thing. But God says *faith* gives access. Don't take this lightly, friend. There is a curse pronounced on anyone who preaches contrary to the righteousness by faith message (Galatians 1:9). That word "curse" is from the Greek *anathema* and essentially means "to set apart for damnation." This means that if you're the type of person who runs an ongoing mental checklist of rules to reassure yourself that you're heaven-bound, you could be hell-bound instead. To attribute justification to anything we are, anything we have, or anything we do is not just legalistic; it's treasonous. Consider this:

"I ask, how can I present this matter as it is? The Lord Jesus imparts all the powers, all the grace, all the penitence, all the inclination, all the pardon of sins, in presenting His righteousness for man to grasp by living faith—which is also the gift of God. If you

would gather together everything that is good and holy and noble and lovely in man and then present the subject to the angels of God as acting a part in the salvation of the human soul or in merit, the proposition would be rejected as treason."[2]

This statement plainly says that our claim to meritorious works would provoke the cry, "Traitor!" from the lips of angels.

Some students of the Bible make a distinction between Spirit-inspired and humanly-inspired works, saying that the former have merit before God. Also treason! "Everything that is good and holy and noble and lovely in man" is Spirit-inspired, because "every good gift is from above" (James 1:17). But this doesn't lend to those works any *saving* merit. Even the purest, most God-led works are valueless before God in procuring for us salvation. The best thing to do is give up, right now and forever, any hope that you will in any way, shape, or form earn righteousness. It is, always has been, and always will be a *gift*.

But while we can do nothing to save ourselves, we can do something to prepare to receive salvation. This can be summarized in three steps— come, repent, receive and believe. (Think: come running right back.)

Come. Jesus said, "Come unto Me, all you who are weary and heavy-laden and I will give you rest" (Matthew 11:28). The only prerequisite listed is that you are weary and heavy-laden, or literally "exhausted with toil and loaded down." Certainly we all qualify. Many believe they must repent *before* they come, but this creates a vicious cycle of defeat as they try to conjure up something that only God can impart. Since only God can make us sorry, we must come as we are or not come at all. "Must the sinner wait until he has repented before he can come to Jesus? Is repentance to be made an obstacle between the sinner and the Savior?"[3]

Repent. According to Peter's sermon in Acts 5:31, God *gives* "repentance . . . and forgiveness of sins." Repentance itself is a gift. Both God's mercy and our capacity to receive it must be received from Him. "We can no more repent without the Spirit of Christ to awaken the conscience than we can be pardoned without Christ."[4]

True repentance is "godly sorrow" (2 Corinthians 7:10) for sin itself, rather than merely the consequences of sin. This others-focused view starves the root of sin, which is selfishness. Empathy replaces self-pity, and love consumes self-centeredness.

Repentance bears fruit in specific, heartfelt confession to both God and others you've hurt. Even Alcoholics Anonymous requires its members to take a "fearless moral inventory" and make amends with those harmed. This step is at times difficult, but the promise is that "If we confess our sins, He is faithful and righteous to forgive our sins and cleanse us from all unrighteousness" (1 John 1:9).

Receive. Repentance creates a space in the soul for the righteousness that would otherwise be wasted. Forgiveness is only meaningful when knowingly undeserved: "Now to one who works, his wage is not reckoned as a favor, but as what is due. But to the one who does not work, but believes in Him who justifies the ungodly, his faith is reckoned as righteousness," (Romans 4:4). The impulse to deserve, the aversion to receiving something undeserved, must be suppressed; this is one "wage" you can't earn. Receive it anyway.

Believe. Alleluia! You're standing justified before God. Now is the time to exercise faith in His promise. Faith is an act of the will in which we renounce our own internal lies, replacing them with truth; "Casting down imaginations, and every high thing that exalts itself against the knowledge of God, and bringing into captivity every thought to the obedience of Christ"; "Be transformed by the renewing of your mind" (2 Corinthians 10:5, AKJV; Romans 12:2). Once thoughts are brought into harmony with God, emotions will gradually mold to them.

There are two mistakes Christians make in this regard. One is an intellectual faith, based on head knowledge, which never moves south to the heart region. Merely to acknowledge the truth with no heart-renewal is worthless, even potentially wicked, because "the devils also believe, and tremble" (James 2:19 AKJV). In reality, a head-knowledge religion is underpinned by unbelief, by deeply-held, often unconscious assumptions that steer the life away from God like the unseen but powerful rudder of a ship. True faith penetrates to the substrata of our consciousness, "for with the *heart* a person believes, resulting in righteousness" (Romans 10:10, emphasis mine).

The second mistake is what in psychology is called "emotional reasoning." It functions through a circular process: We feel guilty, for instance. We then reason, "If I feel guilty, I must *be* guilty. I must not be justified before God." But we've come to Jesus, repented of our sins and made amends to the best of our ability. If, because of our feelings of guilt, we conclude that we *are* guilty, we're regarding our emotions as reliable evidences of reality. Letting emotions steer us is like handing the wheel of a car to a five-year-old. The five-year-old is precious, but not capable of steering. A life of faith can be emotionally rich, or at times as dry as desert sand. Like a schooner, we must set our sails toward God's promise. Then we can sail directly into the winds of emotion and still be propelled home.

"Where is boasting? It is excluded. By what kind of law? Of works? No, but by a law of faith" (Romans 3:28). A works religion allows us to retain our bragging rights, but the third angel's message starves pride down to a gleaming white skeleton by the side of the road. It's time for a funeral, believers in Jesus. It's time to accept the plain truths of God's Word and stand in His righteousness alone.

Endnotes

1) See Luke 18:12.

2) Manuscript 36, 1890.

3) *Steps to Christ*, p. 26.

4) *Ibid.*

Chapter Seven
Faith It Till You Make It

On to the messy business of personal growth in Christ, or what is called "sanctification." One might argue that all this talk of acceptance and love removes the incentive for change. Actually, the opposite is true. Jesus' faith in us is the unmatched motivator for holy living.

I'm well acquainted with a young lady who spent her teen years dissipating with drugs. Failure in school led to expulsion, and she began to see herself as a "bad girl." This led to a downward cycle which ended in full-blown cocaine addiction and polydrug use. Sadly, a rather typical story. But what isn't typical is the way it ended. One night she came home from a party and her mother said the following words: "Angela, you'll die if you don't change, and I don't think you'll change until you accept Jesus." Weary from five straight years of repelling the Holy Ghost, Angela said, "Okay, I'm ready." The two prayed a simple prayer of surrender, and Angela was officially a Christian.

But she had a long battle ahead of her. For one thing, she was a drug addict, and there were physiological hurdles to jump. Secondly, her entire social network had been formed during her party life, so there were social dynamics pulling her down. Finally, her most ferocious opponents were her own thought patterns of unbelief, long held and deeply entrenched.

Angela's parents could see all this, and so kept repeating to her Paul's words, "If any man is in Christ, he is a new creature; the old things passed away; behold new things have come" (2 Corinthians 5:17). Over and over, through valley and height, failure and recovery, these words were repeated. Several times Angela claimed, "I'm not really a Christian because I can't do it. It's too hard!" But Angela's mom and dad would counter with, "God has claims on you. He knows what you will be, and He sees you now as a new creature."

Today Angela is a vibrant, loving (albeit struggling, imperfect) Christian, largely because she leaned on her parents' faith that she was a new creature, even when it didn't appear to be so. The phenomenon at work here is what in psychology is called "identity formation." It's a well-established fact in the field of behavioral science that people tend to become what they think they are.[1] Imagine if that first night Angela's mother had said, "God forgives the past, but He expects you to change now." And then imagine if after Angela's first relapse, Dad piped in with, "I guess you never really changed at all, did you?" They would have dealt a death blow to the basis of Angela's faith by denying God's promise of regeneration.

Notice what God says about Abraham, recorded in Romans 4:20: "He did not waver in unbelief." It almost makes one ask, "Are we talking about the same Abraham?" Abraham's unbelief in producing Ishmael through Hagar is one of the most oft-referenced acts of unbelief in the Bible! And God says He didn't waiver? Does God have amnesia? No, but He does have omniscience. He takes in the big picture. He isn't looking at Abraham's Hagar-lapse when He makes His final assessment of the man. Why? Because Abraham did learn his faith lesson. He finally graduated to "father-of-the-faithful" status, and God applied that final attainment retroactively to his entire life.

You may be thinking, "Yeah, but I have no final victory for God to apply." Oh, but you do. Remember that God knows the end from the beginning and knows the final state of sanctification you will reach in Him. He applies this to your life record now and proclaims you perfectly faithful and victorious. The great I AM doesn't work within the confines of human time and so isn't perturbed by your temporary failure. He sees you as you are in Christ, the final, finished, glorious product of sanctification.

Think about it. What hope would there be for any of us without this? If we had to base our identity on current performance, all we could do to change that identity would be to perform better. But fixing our eyes on our own behavior is, in itself, self-centered. Self-centeredness is sinful. So we wind up trying to overcome self by focusing on self. The classic reactive cycle of legalism results, and it prevents true, healthy character development the way too many ballet lessons ruin a little girl's feet. God's children aren't to be regimented into great performers; they are to grow naturally in the sunshine of their Father's love and acceptance.

It is your privilege as a Christian to *today, now* see yourself as God sees you—"complete in Christ" (Colossians 1:28). Do you choose to accept Jesus? Have you followed the basic steps of come, repent, confess, and believe? If so, your growth in Christ is guaranteed by God's own Word:

"For I am confident of this very thing, that He who has begun a good work in you will complete it until the day of Christ Jesus" (Philppians 1:6, NKJV).

"His divine power has granted to us everything pertaining to life and godliness, through the true knowledge of Him who called us by His own glory and excellence" (2 Peter 1:3).

"I will give you a new heart and put a new spirit within you . . . and cause you to walk in my statutes" (Ezekiel 36:26, 27).

"I will put the fear of Me in their hearts so that they will not turn away from Me" (Jeremiah 32:40).

"It has not appeared as yet what we will be, but we know that when He appears, we will be like Him, because we will see Him just as He is. And everyone who has this hope fixed on Him purifies himself, just as He is pure" (1 John 3: 2, 3).

Mark this point: *It is your privilege as a believer in Jesus to regard every departure from Christlike behavior as a temporary lapse into your old life rather than a self-defining act.*

Again, self-image, self-identity, is recognized by psychologists to be a powerful motivator. The Babylonian psychologists knew this, too, which is why they changed the names of Daniel and his friends to Babylonian names. For instance, Daniel means "judged by God" in Hebrew; but his Babylonian name, *Bel*teshazzar refers to the Babylonian god Bel. The enemy employs the same tactics today, attempting to distract you from your true identity in Christ.

The greatest assault on this identity is our own failures—especially addictive, compulsive, repeated sin. Typically these sins are private, lurking behind closed doors long after we've reformed our public lives. Sexual sin, substance abuse, and eating disorders are some of the big culprits. Many a Christian wrestles with their power to the point of despair. Dizzied by the cycle of sin and repentance, they are ready to jump out of their faith into full-blown unbelief.

Such people should remember that to sin and repent is better than to sin and *not* repent! There may be a period of defeat before the final victory, but "let endurance have its perfect result, that you may be perfect and complete, lacking in nothing" (James 1:4). "He that endures to the end" is the one who endures discouragement over his own sinfulness, but continues to trust in God's promise. Yes, God wants us to stop sinning (1 John 2:1), but He can use even our falls for our sanctification. Sometimes a temporary lack of victory over behavioral sin can serve to excise the deeper, more problematic sin of spiritual pride.

Yes, God wishes "that we should not sin," but let's not forget that "if anyone sins, we have an advocate with the Father, Jesus Christ the righteous" (1 John 2:1). We can conceptualize this twofold reality as a baby learning to walk. With each attempt, she works off two assumptions— that she will someday walk, and that she may fall on the way to walking. Again, her basic assumptions are, *I will walk*, and *I may fall*. If the baby denied the first assumption, she'd lose the hope of walking. If she denied the second assumption, she'd lose the courage to try. Like this toddling little one, we need to tell ourselves the truth about walking with Jesus:

I will walk. The promise is that "sin shall not be master over you," and that He is "able to keep you from stumbling" (Romans 6:14; Jude 1:24). Some cite their past failure as evidence that they can't change. There's validity to this belief—humanly speaking, it's true. The unaided human will is powerless to conquer deep-rooted sin; the demoniacs couldn't cast out their own demons. But they could choose Christ, who did the casting-out *for* them. In conquering cultivated habits of sin, a blending of divine grace and human choice is the only potent weapon. We're powerless in the face of besetting sin, but not powerless to cast ourselves on Jesus' power:

"You cannot change your heart, you cannot of yourself give to God its affections; but you can *choose* to serve Him. You can give Him your will; He will then work in you to will and to do according to His good pleasure."[2]

Don't wait until you have a perfect understanding of how this choosing takes place. We learn kinesthetically, by doing. I call this "faith it till you make it." Believing that self-mastery is ours in Christ, we act in accordance. Our actions reflectively mold our emotions, creating an internal environment to match our choice. Neuroscience confirms the brain's "plasticity," that is, its ability to change, and how action and thought mirror one another. God has proclaimed you to be a new creature in Christ. Convince yourself of this by acting on His Word.

Many are like the snake-bitten children of Israel, forever examining their wounds. They overidentify with their past failures, saying, "Look at my history! I'll never change!" The problem with this thinking is that the past has never been a good predictor of the future. "Behold, I will do something new; now it will spring forth. Will you not be aware of it?" (Isaiah 43:19). True, the momentum of repeated sin builds upon itself; conditions can appear hopeless when one is entangled in a string of failures. But God is the Master Untangler. Get up right now and walk, believing that He will free your feet.

I may fall. Some feel that to admit the possibility of falling is a form of license. Such need to understand that we can be honest about sin without approving of it. Frankness and common sense about human nature can actually fortify us against temptation; denial only makes us blind and vulnerable. Besides, denied sins don't disappear any faster than unpaid taxes do! A goody-goody self-image is a very brittle and fragile thing that makes a soul intolerant to reality. Why be shocked when sinners *sin*?

The first week after my conversion, in the absence of clear teaching on the gospel, I came to the conclusion that if I fell into sin again, I'd be lost. It was the most stressful week of my life! Thank God that the woman who led me to Christ set me straight, or I would have soon caved in to despair. And here is an important point: apathy would have followed. Perfectionism wears out the spirit to the point of collapse. Listen to the wise man: "Do not be *excessively righteous* and do not be overly wise. Why should you *ruin yourself*?" (Ecclesiastes 7:16, italics supplied). "Excessive" righteousness is ruinous! In psychology we call it *hypervigilance,* and we know it to pave the way for indifference. The nervous system simply burns out from all the worry. This is why Ellen White said, "Excess of caution is often attended with as great danger as excess of confidence."[3] We should be concerned about the creeping compromise, but equally concerned about the bouncing boomerang.

I will walk, but I may fall. This is God's foolproof method of sanctification. Here it is in the words of inspiration: "To go forward without stumbling, we must have the assurance that a hand all-powerful will hold us up, and an infinite pity be exercised toward us if we fall."[4]

Proud parents coax and cheer as their baby attempts her first steps. They know she will walk—they have faith in the developmental process. Down she tumbles over and over, but they simply help her stand and urge her forward again and again until, one day, she walks without falling. Believer in Jesus, God knows you'll walk some day. Fly to Him when you fall, and He will help you up. Believe that He can give you the grace to walk without falling, and when He comes again, you will fly into His arms.

Endnotes

1) For instance, "identity variables contributed significantly and independently to the explanation of behavioral intentions," from Pierro, Mannetti and Livi, "Self and Self-Identity," *Psychology Press,* 2: 1, pp. 47.

2) *Steps to Christ,* p. 47.

3) *Signs of the Times,* July 28, 1881.

4) *Ibid.*

Chapter Eight
The Sanctuary, My Refuge

My friend Trina and I had a two-woman mutual admiration society. Both singer/songwriters, we swapped songs, shared producers and sang background vocals for each other. She thought I was a great songwriter, once even crying while I played her a new song. "I'm not crying because the song was sad," she sniffed, "but because I didn't write it!" My admiration for Trina was mutual. She was a winner of a girl with her good looks, gorgeous voice, and bubbly personality.

Hundreds of people were disappointed when Trina sent out a letter informing us that she was leaving the Adventist church. Her core reason was that she no longer believed the church's teaching on what is called the investigative judgment.

Here is a brief synopsis of that teaching:

The preaching of William Miller in the early 1800s revived thousands with the message of Jesus' soon coming. Miller had studied the prophecies of Daniel, which revealed a timeline that ended at 1844—the time of Jesus' return, or so he thought. Because of his message, committed believers sold their homes and waited. But Jesus never came. We call this the Great Disappointment for obvious reasons.

Still clinging to the faith that God had led them, Miller's band went back to their Bibles and discovered their mistake. It was a false assumption about Daniel 8:14: "Unto two thousand and three hundred days; then shall the sanctuary be cleansed." They had assumed that the sanctuary was the *earth*, which was a popular interpretation at the time. The timeline Miller had mapped out ended the at coming of Jesus, when the earth, or "the sanctuary" would be cleansed by the brightness of His glory. Upon reexamination, the group realized that they were right about the time, but wrong about the event; it was the sanctuary in *heaven* that was being cleansed.

Stay with me through a little more detail. The earthly sanctuary was "made after a pattern" (Hebrews 8:5) shown to Moses. It was God's show-and-tell of the sanctuary in heaven. A yearly national fast was commanded (see Leviticus 16), during which the people of Israel mourned their collective sins. During this "day of atonement" the high priest symbolically moved the sin from the outer compartment to the inmost compartment where the presence of God was revealed in the Shekinah—a searingly brilliant manifestation of God's glory. This was a service so solemn that the high priest ran the risk of being struck dead, did he carry any unconfessed sin. Once the high priest made atonement, the sins of Israel were symbolically moved from the sanctuary to the wilderness through a scapegoat. In this way the earthly sanctuary was symbolically cleansed of the sin that had compiled throughout the year. Essentially, it was a sin-disposal system.

As the Millerites studied this teaching, they realized that before Jesus could come, God's heavenly tabernacle would undergo the same "housekeeping" process. This, they realized, was the significant event that would begin in 1844. The lives of God's people were being scrutinized, one by one, beginning with the dead and moving on to the living. Adventists have since named this the "investigative judgment" because the saints' lives are *investigated* to discern whether or not their profession is genuine.

The nature of this book prevents me from giving an extensive, technical defense of this doctrine. What I want to posit is why it even matters. The brief answer is that the investigative judgment is God's end-time method of solemnizing the experience of His followers. Contrary to popular sentiments, a little judgment and heart-searching benefit us, especially in times when deceptions are at their most seductive.

Think about the stumbling blocks that professed Christians have strewn before the feet of non-believers. Self-satisfied, sassy, entitlement-spirited religionists misrepresent the humble Jesus daily, their double lives eventually exposed and broadcast through the media. Yet this is no new phenomenon. Professed Christianity put the "dark" in the Dark Ages. From the medieval knight slaughtering Muslims and Jews in Christ's name to the morality-touting, politically-motivated media Christian who secretly patronizes the sex industry we see example after example of "whited sepulchers" who "appear beautiful" but are full of death (see Matthew 23:27). Does the blood of Jesus cover such compromise? Does His robe of righteousness cloak such corruption? A thousand times no. What is hidden will be made known, and the investigative judgment makes sure of it.

It is for *our* good, and the good of our universe, in these sunset hours of earth's history, that we have a time of reflection on what sin has cost our Savior. Presumption has stained history as professors of religion have lusted, cheated, stolen, maimed and killed in the name of God. The investigative judgment puts the conscience back in Christianity.

This provokes a reaction of resentment in some. The idea of believers undergoing scrutiny seems out of harmony with the "no condemnation" pronounced on those who "are in Christ" (Romans 8:1). Yet all are judged by works,[1] and this poses no threat to salvation by grace through faith. Works give evidence of faith the way the smell of cookies reveal something good in the oven. The investigative judgment reveals what's cooking in the lives of believers. There's nothing unhealthy about such accountability if it's gospel-based.

But I must pause to balance this out a little, admitting as an Adventist that fear-based religion has sometimes twisted the investigative judgment doctrine into an ideological monster. After all, the enemy cares not whether we fall into the ditch of presumption or legalism, as long as we fall. Conscience has, at times, degenerated into condemnation. I have known many insecure souls who lived in a state of anxiety that was more appropriate for a police state than the religion of Christ. I'm probably the best illustration of this; a fear-based religion helped me develop an eating disorder as a new believer. Anorexia kept me weak and innocuous when, as a young person, sex drive was the number one threat to my purity. My unconscious strategy for sinlessness was to starve myself down to 95 pounds, putting my body in survival mode. Chronic low blood sugar served to subdue the bolder aspects of my personality. Solemn, somber, and quiet, I thought I was holy. In reality, I was hungry.

Fear has its place, but when fear is maintained for long periods without maturing into reverential love, the result is spiritual breakdown. This is why the doctrine of eternally burning hell is so insidious—it produces "millions of skeptics and infidels."[2] In the same way, the fear-based perversion of the investigative judgment has led many to shun the idea entirely.

Is it possible to teach something as serious as the judgment of the living without triggering a prolonged fight or flight reaction? Yes, but the gospel of God, rather than the performance of man, must be nailed to the center. When our attempts to overcome sin spring from self-interest, the attempts themselves become sin, because, "every action derives its quality from the motive which prompts it."[3] Think for a moment about the sheer idiocy of self-centered perfectionism—it's selfish "sinlessness." That's about as incongruous as greedy generosity or lustful purity. It's an oxymoron, a contradiction in terms and an impossibility.

This problem is solved, however, when we look at the sin problem through a different colored lens. When the declaratives of the gospel, and the acceptance of those gifts by faith, free us from insecurity, we can bear up under God's scrutiny without fear. There is something much bigger than our own salvation and happiness at stake. We see sin in the context of the great controversy, and it takes on a different hue. The focus shifts to:

Jesus. No longer are our attempts to put away sin a self-purging penance, but a love-motivated desire to cooperate with Christ in His sacred work. For love of country, soldiers lay down their lives. For love of heavenly country, Christian soldiers also forget themselves, swept up in the cosmic battle. They sing, "Great and marvelous are Your works, Lord God Almighty! Just and true are Your ways, O King of the saints!" (Revelation 15:3, NKJV). This is called the "song of Moses and the Lamb." Remember that both Moses and Christ were willing to lay down their own salvation for the sake of others and God (see Exodus 32:32 and 2 Corinthians 5:21). Their obsession was not over their place in the kingdom, but over the kingdom itself, and ultimately over the King. Similarly, the end-time believers fear that they have unconfessed sins; yet their concern is not their own souls, but that "God's holy name would be reproached."[4]

The Body. Separatist perfectionism leads people to fear being tainted by fellowship with Laodicea because it is filled with "worldly" people. But this fear of infection is . . . an infection. "Ultraconservative" separatists should add "fellowship" to their to-do list if they're so concerned about obedience! Unity with God's people is just as much a command as separation from the world's principles.[5]

The depth of our commitment to the Head is tested by our love for the body. Jesus will lead us "till we *all* come to the unity of the faith and of the knowledge of the Son of God, to a perfect man, to the measure of the stature of the fullness of Christ" (Ephesians 4:13, NKJV, emphasis mine). Notice that "we all" in "unity" produce "a perfect man." We are only as perfect as our unselfish commitment to the body, not saved in groups, but grown in relationship one to another.

What a relief to be released from pathetic self-concern to the freedom of sinking my heart into the grand issues of the cosmic conflict between Christ and Satan! What a privilege to be invested in a cause so much bigger than myself. The human heart longs to be part of something cosmic, outsized, and expansive. Well, this is it. God has given us a supporting role in the great drama of the ages.

The investigative judgment proves God's goodness, not our own. It showcases His power in human lives. Heaven and earth wait to see whether God's love can transform humanity back into His image. "For the earnest expectation of the creation eagerly waits for the revealing of the sons of God" (Romans 8:19, NKJV). The toughest "road test" for God's grace has been the narcissistic human heart. Can even *that* test be passed? The final cleansing of the sanctuary in heaven says it can.

The investigative judgment has not imprisoned me in fear, but delivered me from it. The sanctuary has been a refuge from the tortures of selfish religion. True security in Christ is like a butterfly; the more you chase it, the more it eludes you. How much better to make our security His concern, and His witness in the earth our concern.

Endnotes

1) Matthew 16:27 says, "For the Son of Man is going to come in the glory of His Father with His angels; and will then recompense every man according to his deeds." Romans 2:6 says God will "render to every man according to his deeds." 2 Corinthians 5:10 says, "For we must all appear before the judgment seat of Christ, that each one may be recompensed for his deeds in the body, according to what he has done, whether good or bad." Finally, Revelation 20:12 says, "And I saw the dead, both great and the small, standing before the throne, and books were opened and another book was opened, which is the book of life; and the dead were judged from the things which were written in the books, according to their deeds."

2) *The Great Controversy*, p. 536.

3) *Youth's Instructor,* April 7, 1898.

4) *Ibid.*, p. 619.

5) See 1 Cor. 14; Ro. 12:1-13; Eph. 4:1-16; Eph. 2:19-22.

Chapter Nine
Lessons from Boot Camp

Dad had been in pain for a long time when finally a physician ordered an MRI. It was the worst possible news—cancer. And it was the worst possible cancer—pancreatic.

Pancreatic cancer. I hate those words.

Dad had an almost unsinkable faith in modern medicine. "We're gonna try to lick this thing," he said, "first with surgery, then with chemo, then radiation . . . I know a fella who had pancreatic cancer . . . he's doin' pretty good." Candid physician friends weren't nearly so hopeful. Pancreatic cancer patients, if diagnosed early, may live five years if they're lucky, and Dad wasn't diagnosed early.

My sister and I drove eighteen hours straight to see him after his first operation. A funny quandary these surgeries present—you may remove the cancer, but then you may help the cancer remove you. Cancer cells are just clumps of overoxidized tissue to begin with, so when the body is opened up to the air, one hopes that the benefits will outweigh the risks. In Dad's case, they didn't.

Nine months later he informed us that he was dying. None of us believed him, because he was still walking around, functioning, talking. He called the family in from Connecticut, Massachusetts, Texas, and Kansas to come bid him farewell. On Sabbath we gathered together around his bed, where he was propped up like a rag doll. His once-athletic form was bloated beyond recognition, and what was left of his brown hair had blanched and frizzed into little white puffs behind his ears. As we gazed into his watery old eyes, we knew we'd been called to a sacred event. "I wanted to tell you all how much I love you," our patriarch began, "and I want you to know I realize some things . . . " His little speech began with his own amend-making and turned into three hours of family catharsis. We reminisced, laughed till we cried, said goodbye, and cried again. After Dad had pronounced his "blessing" upon the family, he lay down, never to rise, eat, or talk again in this world.

Although he attended church with Mom, my conversion mystified Dad. When my sister converted to Adventism, things went from confused to devastating. Kristin was his favorite child and Adventism his least favorite religion. As an act of protest to Kristin's conversion, Dad stopped attending church with my mom, fuming mad at the God he didn't believe in. Was he still mad? I didn't know. As he lay dying, I felt the urge to talk to him about salvation, but it felt awkward. This appeal, I knew, would be a God-thing, not a Jennifer-thing. My window of opportunity arrived only hours before he breathed his last. It was my shift at his bedside, so I played my guitar softly for him as a warm wind blew. The Spirit of God spoke: "Now is the time."

"Dad," I whispered, "You haven't been a very religious man, but God still has a mansion prepared for you in heaven. You want to see us all again, Dad; I know you do. You can! Just say in your mind, 'Jesus, I accept You,' and you can be saved. Just believe, Dad, right now, and we can all meet together in eternity. Follow along with me as I pray. . ." I looked up at dad's agony-lined face and noticed streaming tears. He was unable to talk, but clearly able to hear and process my words.

When all a person has left are a few synaptic connections in the brain, when all electrical impulses to the body and mouth have failed, can God still honor the silent "Yes"? If you'd asked me that as a young Christian, I may not have been able to answer in the affirmative. But by the time my dad passed off the scene, the gospel had thankfully stretched my heart to understand that Jesus could "save them to the uttermost who come to God by Him" (Hebrews 7:25, KJV).

Dad had been very turned off by Adventism, mostly because of the extremism of my early experience. It's not that I was unconverted as a young Christian; it's that I was like the children of Israel under the old covenant.

I had enthusiastically committed myself to obey God's standards, saying in my inmost heart, "All that thou hast said I will do." Accordingly, I felt pressured to convert everyone around me, since witnessing was also one of God's dictates. As a result, every other comment I made declared the virtues of veganism, Sabbath-keeping, tithing, church membership, Ellen White, and Bible study. This I did with less tact than a two-year-old, and then was puzzled when friends and family members recoiled. It was as if I'd lost my personableness. Witnessing, for me, was another item on the to-do list, fulfilled dutifully and efficiently. Relationships? What were they? It was information that mattered. These people needed to be warned, not related to.[1]

Truth be told, this erratic approach was the fruit of fear. New in my commitment to right living, I gathered the standards around me like a fortress. But externalized standards become rigid rules that can only protect against the behavioral aspect of sin, which problem penetrates far beyond behavior to all aspects of our being. God is willing to send us to bootcamp as a means of taming our most self-destructive habits, but bootcamp should be temporary. Ideally and eventually, we *internalize* God's principles. Then our fear of relapse is replaced by the love in which there is no fear (1 John 4:18). This internalizing process is what distinguishes the new covenant from the old.

Let's get our bearings on this issue of the covenants. The old covenant (also called the "first" covenant) came about after God had miraculously delivered Israel from Egypt. While encamping at Sinai, Moses was called to the mountain to meet with God, who was establishing Himself as the theocratic Head of Israel. "You yourselves have seen what I did to the Egyptians," He said, "and how I bore you on eagles' wings, and brought you to Myself. Now, then, if you will indeed obey [Hebrew "shama" means "listen"] My voice and keep [Hebrew "shamar" means "guard"] My covenant, then you shall be My own possession among all the peoples, for all the earth is Mine; and you shall be to Me a kingdom of priests and a holy nation" (Exodus 19:4-6). What a promise! God essentially said:

I flew you out of the land of slavery.
Keep listening and don't throw away my covenant.
I'll make a holy, happy nation out of you.

As tenderly as God spoke these words, unconverted ears heard:

I've helped you out.
But now I expect you to pay me back by keeping my rules.
If you do, I'll make you powerful.
The human response to this covenant was a vow:
"All that the Lord has spoken we will do!" (Exodus 19:8).

Back into the mountain Moses climbed, emerging after three days. To the trembling people he spoke the Ten Commandments, and because their slavery-blunted synapses couldn't grasp those divine principles, a set of additional precepts called "the ceremonial law" were given. Through these precepts God explained how His law would factor out in every minute facet of life. The awestruck people again promised:

"All the words which the Lord has spoken we will do!" (Exodus 24:3). "All that the Lord has spoken we will do, and we will be obedient!" (Exodus 24:7).

Within days the goody-goodies were dancing naked around a golden calf!

What made the old covenant ineffective wasn't God; it was the people's response. Their can-do confidence was actually a form of denial and served to repel God's grace rather than absorb it. Likewise, conservative Adventists often exhibit an air of self-reliance, not realizing that the very prophet whose standards they idealize said that wherever "the principle that man can save himself by His own works" is held, "men have no barrier against sin."[2] Don't we all have our own little golden-calf reminders of this? Our "promises and resolutions are like ropes of sand."[3] We may see something of God's power and holiness, but if our hearts aren't captured by His love, we are at best well-intentioned and weak-willed idolators.

It's ironic that "old covenant" has the same initials as "obsessive-compulsive." Obsessive-compulsive disorder is an anxiety disorder which involves ritualistic observances such as hand-washing or repeatedly locking doors. Similarly, old-covenant religion is fear-motivated and compulsive. The fear instilled by an encounter with God's holiness is a good start for our Christian experience, but a very bad place to get stuck. Thank God there is a better way, a new covenant.

Hebrews 8:10-12 explains it this way:

"For this is the covenant that I will make with the house of Israel after those days, says the Lord. I will put My laws into their minds, and I will write them upon their hearts; and I will be their God, and they shall be My people. And they shall not teach everyone his fellow citizen, and everyone his brother, saying, 'Know the Lord,' for all shall know Me, from the least to the greatest of them. For I will be merciful to their iniquities, and I will remember their sins no more."

How does the new covenant differ from the old? Let's break it down from this passage:

It's internal versus external. Psychology's best-known expert on moral development was Lawrence Kohlberg, who observed that the most primal of motivations was fear of punishment. Next was hope of reward. As a baby matured into a child, spankings and lollypops were replaced by social incentives, adapting the punishment/reward system but not changing it essentially. Only at the most advanced stage of development—called "post conventional"—were humans motivated by internally embedded principles as opposed to external consequences. Kohlberg had keen insights into human nature, but his theory raises the question as to how this internalization takes place. Thankfully, our Divine

Psychotherapist goes beyond describing the process—He provides the power. He Himself will "put" His laws into our minds and "write" them upon our hearts.

It's personal versus theoretical. Like the Ph.D. in aquatics who can't swim, old-covenant believers are book-smart and street-stupid. They sound good, as six-year-olds obliviously reciting the Pledge of Allegiance sound good. So what? Seminars, sermons, books, and studies proliferate—but to what end? We may know the facts about Jesus, but do we know *Him*? The Biblical words for "know" convey deep intimacy: "This is life eternal, that they may *know* You" John 17:3. Moreover, while academic learning tends to engender competition, intimacy with Christ equalizes believers as they meet on level ground at the foot of the Cross. "Knowledge makes arrogant, but love edifies" (1 Corinthians 8:1).

It's transformational versus behavioral .Behavioral therapy has a high relapse rate, simply because it fails to change underlying cognitions and motivations. Many are the old-covenant souls who become like well-trained seals balancing balls on their noses. They are behaviorally skilled, but emotionally and relationally dwarfed. The old covenant shapes behavior from the outside, but the new covenant introduces forgiveness and heart cleansing, which redirect heart, mind, soul, and body toward heaven.

There's a place for the behavioral modification. Through a quick reformation of our outward actions, boot camp can save us from self-destructive acting out. Likewise, there's a place for the old covenant, or God wouldn't have instituted it. But the kindergarten mentality that naively promises obedience must mature into heart-obedience or we'll find ourselves stuck in a religion of externals. Human promises must give way to God's promise to put His laws into our minds and write them on our hearts. Then His commandments themselves become promises, assurances that under His new covenant, our lives will change because our hearts and minds have changed. Amen.

Endnotes

1 I'm exaggerating a little, but only a little.

2 *Desire of Ages*, p. 35.

3 *Steps to Christ*, p. 47.

Chapter Ten
"You're No Better"

I have a history of skepticism toward marriage seminars, especially the method-driven kind. Some of the techniques described have seemed to mock the depth of relationship wounds, like a band-aid fails to bind a deep gash: little love notes in the lunch box., twelve meaningful touches a day, fighting fair. These things can be helpful, but they don't replace the work only God can do. How can something as manmade as a *technique* undertake something as supernatural as the spiritual union of two sinners?

I once watched some friends present one such seminar. They looked so sparklingly happy up there. I appreciated this couple's commitment to each other, but their marriage was young, they had no children, and their financial pressures were nil. Another presentation by a man included multiple sighs and romantic remarks about his absolutely gorgeous wife. I scanned the crowd, empathizing with the homely people who were probably assuming they could never have such bliss because they didn't have such looks. Yet another man spoke of his affectionate treatment of his wife in very white-knightly terms until I sensed that the women there were starting to wish they were married to *him*. In all of these scenarios, I failed to get the help intended because I believed that these people somehow had superior *equipment* to mine, that their marriage worked because they had more of some mysterious love-juice. The more "encouragement" I got from these "good" marriages, the less accessible a "good" marriage became.

What finally made sense for me was to discard the idea of a good marriage. Anecdotal evidence proved me right when some of these model marriages unraveled before my eyes. Then there were the marriages that seemed destined to fail still putt-putting along after decades. My own might be included in that category. Neither my husband nor I have ever entertained the idea of legal divorce, but we have had a few psychological divorces over the years. Yet is seems that however embattled our bond, it has outlasted prettier marriages, marriages with better forecasts.

I must give the gospel credit for this. Specifically, I must acknowledge that one simple gospel principle has kept our marriage off the dunghill of divorce. That principle can be boiled down into a simple sentence, spoken by the Holy Spirit to my heart on a daily basis: "You're no better than him." Speaking for myself, the core belief that needed to be routed out of my thinking was that I was somehow superior to my spouse, that I was the big one in the marriage, the one who settled for less, the martyr, the saint. This sense of superiority is basic to human nature, and marriage is often the place where it has its most purulent expression.[1]

One of the things that makes this "stinking thinking" possible is the fact that sin comes in a variety pack. A wife has one variety, while her spouse has another. I suppose in this sense my marriage was the epitome of the adage that "opposites attract" in that we didn't even have similar *sins.* When I wanted to win an argument, I would mention his sins and feel very self-righteous indeed because I didn't fall on those points. That was all well and good until he did the same thing and pointed out my sins, which he wasn't tempted by at all. When *he* then felt self-righteous, there were two people under the same roof feeling holier-than-thou, and let me assure you, there is a no more miserable state of existence.

Honesty about our total lack of righteousness is a better option.

Much of the success of Alcoholics Anonymous is due to this honesty. Members all have the same addiction, and therefore no one is able to feel superior to others. No drunk can say of another's drunken binge, "I would never do that!" It is God's will that the church foster that same kind of honesty. While each has their distinctive struggles, there should be a recognition that "all have sinned and fall short of the glory of God" (Romans 3:23). The problem is, our distance vision is good enough to see the sins of those far away from us, but "presbyopia"[2] blurs things right in front of our eyes, such as our own shortcomings. This is why we need "'eye salve ... that [we] may see'" (Revelation 3:18).

Okay, back up a little. Aren't some of God's children quite the opposite—prone to blame themselves and excuse others? True, the weak consciences of these people (who are often victims of abuse) lead them to personalize everything, subjugating their will to stronger minds, taking responsibility for sins not their own. But this is just inverted self-righteousness. These guilt-ridden ones are, in an indirect way, attempting to soothe away their shame by surrendering their consciences to another. This isn't true humility, but it sometimes passes for it.

It's ironic that self-righteousness had its nativity in the first marriage on planet Earth (marriage ever since then has proven to be a perfect breeding ground for it). Adam and Eve, when they began to realize their lost condition, hid behind fig leaves that represent "the arguments used to cover disobedience."[3] They had never known guilt, and now it threatened to engulf them. They then did what human beings typically do to deflect guilt—they manufactured their own righteousness.

I can't blame them, for guilt is a deadly thing. In fact, it was our guilt that crushed out the life of Jesus on the cross when He was "slain by the sin of the world."[4] No one in their right mind wants to walk into the jaws of condemnation. Human beings are created with a powerful self-preservation instinct that readily multiplies defense mechanisms under duress. We must have righteousness from some source, and in the absence of Christ's righteousness we will contrive our own.

Now, watch what happened to the original marriage. Once they fig-leafed their own righteousness, they began to blame one another, for when we attempt to ward off responsibility, it must go somewhere. When God finally confronted them, their relationship had completely disintegrated. Remember, Adam thought that God was coming to destroy him (see Genesis 2:17). When Adam was sure he was about to be executed, he attempted to hoodwink the Lord into thinking that Eve was the culprit, hoping that God would execute her and spare him. So soon after "loving" Eve enough to make her his idol, he was *unloving* enough to make her his scapegoat. This ridiculous shift occurred in *one day!* Such is the volatility of human love.

Ever since the Fall, self-righteousness and blame have been an essential part of human nature. Social psychology identifies these tendencies. "Fundamental attribution bias" is the well-documented tendency of human beings to attribute other people's misfortunes to those people's own mistakes versus situational factors. On the other hand, "actor-observer bias" is the often-noted phenomenon that "people are more likely to attribute their own behaviors to situational factors than dispositional ones."[5] Illustrated, these traits might look like this: When I see *you* fall, I say, "What a clod!" When *I* fall, I say, "I tripped on that rock!" These two phenomena mean that science has now confirmed what God pointed out through His Word in ages past—that our natural tendency is to blame others and excuse ourselves.

Faced with sin in the lives of friends, enemies, and spouses (which can be either), we react in two ways: disassociation or identity. Disassociation leads us to express shock, "[Gasp!] They did *that*?" The sentiment behind the shock is "I would never do that! I can't even relate to it!" Jesus pointed out to the religious leaders of the day that they would "build the tombs of the prophets and adorn the monuments of the righteous," piously claiming that "'If we had lived in the days of our fathers, we would not have been partakers with them in the blood of the prophets'" (Matthew 23:29-36). Jesus then predicted that they would indeed kill, crucify, and scourge the prophets, scribes, and wise men that He sent them. Thus He draws an inextricable link between the denial of the fathers' sins and the repetition of them. Jesus, the all-knowing divine Psychologist, masterfully connects the Pharisaic blind-spot with falling into the *very sin denied!*

Even great men of faith shared this blind-spot syndrome:

Gideon defeated Midian but manifested a spirit of retaliation toward some neutral cities (Judges 8:16, 17) and eventually led Israel into idolatry (v. 26, 27).

Jehu was mightily used of God in eradicating Baal worship from Israel but never quite left idolatry himself (2 Kings 10:31).

King Josiah was a great reformer in Judah and Jerusalem but would not listen to a heathen king when God spoke through him, resulting in his own death (2 Chronicles 35:20-22).

As with Gideon, Jehu, and Josiah, our success-sated pride is liable to block the view of our personal danger. God takes a great risk in giving us victory at all; we are so prone to misapply it! Fortunately, the Word is filled with blunt, plain-spoken warnings of the depravity of human nature:

Psalms 51:5: "Behold, I was brought forth in iniquity, and in sin did my mother conceive me."

Ecclesiastes 7:20: "Surely there is not a righteous man on earth who does good and never sins."

Ecclesiastes 9:3: "The hearts of the children of men are full of evil, and madness is in their hearts while they live."

Jeremiah 17:9: "The heart is deceitful above all things, and desperately sick; who can understand it?"

Jeremiah 13:23: (NIV): "Can the Ethiopian change his skin or the leopard its spots? Neither can you do good, who are accustomed to doing evil."

Mark 7:21-23: "For from within, out of the heart of man, come evil thoughts, sexual immorality, theft, murder, adultery, coveting, wickedness, deceit, sensuality, envy, slander, pride, foolishness. All these evil things come from within, and they defile a person."

John 8:34: "Jesus answered them, 'Truly, truly, I say to you, everyone who commits sin is a slave to sin.'"

Romans 3:10-11: "None is righteous, no, not one; no one understands; no one seeks for God."

It's hard for believers to admit to madness, murder, adultery, deceit, and slavery; but according to revelation, those capabilities reside within us all. The degree of *development* of evil differs from person to person; the *potential* for evil is the same. This recognition of potential puts to death our innate self-justifying pride. Waggoner said:

"Since all men are alike sharers in one common human nature, it is evident that whosoever in the world condemns another for any misdeed thereby condemns himself; for the truth is that all have the same evil in them, more or less fully developed."[6]

Through the gospel the well-trained, refined, self-disciplined Christian may look across the table at the drunk who wallows in the consequences of genes, circumstances, and the momentum of thousands of poor choices and say, "I'm no better." At the foot of the cross is a level playing field where none can boast, for all must look up and see the One they crucified, the evidence of their depravity. Amazingly, this place where no self-exaltation can flourish is exactly where the delicate plant of love can thrive between human beings.

Does this understanding rule out accountability? Should I totally ignore sin in others because I recognize my capability to commit the same? No, in fact, the recognition of my own potential is the only thing that gives me the proper basis to confront sin in others. "Brethren, if a man is overtaken in any trespass, you who are spiritual restore such a one in a spirit of gentleness, considering yourself lest you also be tempted" (Galatians 6:1, NKJV).

Notice that my motive is to "restore such a one." By ignoring serious sin in the lives of those within my influence, I am missing an opportunity to *restore* them. Rather, Jesus would have us seek the deliverance of those for whom He died. But we are to do it in a "spirit of gentleness," divested of the least hint of self-righteousness, that our desire to help might shine through to their hearts. It is the opposite, mean-spirited approach that has impelled some to automatically associate any judgment of behavior with judgmental*ism*.

Grasping by faith the righteousness of Jesus, self-righteousness is displaced, crowded out of the heart. Guilt-avoidance pathology is disarmed by the knowledge that Jesus' merits are applied to our account. As we begin to rest in His righteousness, we find courage to face ourselves, for "perfect love casts out fear," (1 John 4:18). Just to the degree that we receive freely from Him, we give freely to others.

Marriage seminars? The best ones address the tendency toward self-righteousness and blame, a tendency that first appeared in Eden and has affected each marriage since. God has convinced me that in essence, I am no different from my spouse. Remarkably, this has made all the difference in the world.

Christ's righteousness leads me to see myself as the chief of sinners.

Self-righteousness leads me to feel holier-than-thou.

Christ's righteousness gives me permission to be honest about my sinfulness.

Self-righteousness leaves me in denial.

Christ's righteousness leads me to release guilt as I confess my sin.

Self-righteousness leads me to avoid guilt as I cover up my sin.

Christ's righteousness leads me to lay down my life as He laid down His.

Self-righteousness leads me to go to great lengths in self-preservation.

Christ's righteousness motivates me to lovingly seek to restore the fallen.

Self-righteousness leads me to either ignore or censure the fallen.

Christ's righteousness is received at the cross.

Self-righteousness is expressed by nailing Jesus to it.

Endnotes

1) I'm simplifying here. Some people do the opposite of blaming—they personalize, or take responsibility for other's sins. The potential for this is greater when there is a power imbalance, such as adult-child, or when there is emotional, physical, or sexual abuse. This chapter is meant for a relationship of equals.

2) Presbyopia is what happens to aging eyes when they can't read close up anymore, and they say, "I'm not getting older; my arms are just getting shorter!" then finally go buy those fifteen-dollar reading glasses from Wal-Mart.

3) *Review and Herald,* June 4, 1901.

4) *Desire of Ages*, p. 772.

5) Association for Advanced Training in Behavioral Sciences, *National Counselor,* v. 1, p. 74.

6) Ellet Waggoner, *Waggoner On Romans*, 2.39, 2.40.

Chapter Eleven
Forgiveness, Forgiveness, Trust

For years I tried to forgive a certain individual, and for years failed. What makes betrayal so hard to bear is the baseline of trust one begins with. Deep trust means deep pain when trust is broken. Michael Card put it into words for me one day:

"Only a friend can betray a friend, a stranger has nothing to gain And only a friend comes close enough to ever cause so much pain."[1]

I had let a friend come close, and it caused "so much pain"! Now what would I do with this sense of unfinished business, this lack of closure, this cognitive dissonance? My human attempts at bestowing forgiveness always resulted in a sentimental, surface "reconciliation" with the person, who would soon relapse into old patterns, which would find me hurt and angry. Finally, out of ideas, I decided to make a special effort to study the issue of forgiveness from the Bible. It was a little like *finally* plugging in the toaster after hours of trying to "fix" it, but better late than never.

The Word showed me that merely overlooking the problem was actually worsening it. Denying the seriousness of sin wasn't making it disappear. Like lava beneath the earth's crust, resentment always came bursting forth eventually. I had been trying to extinguish Mount Vesuvius with a watering can.

If we think carefully about this, we realize that the cross speaks to the fact that sin can't be merely overlooked or excused. If it could, why in the world would God have sent His Son to die a horrific death? Unnecessary pain is not God's gig, so to speak. No, but sin blocked the flow of forgiveness until the cross "removed every objection, and put aside everything that would interpose between man and God's pardoning love."[2]

Does the fact that the cross was necessary for forgiveness indicate a grudge-bearing on God's part? Some characterize the idea of substitution, portraying a testosterone-loaded deity, fists clenched, desperate to beat on someone—anyone—to vent His rage over sin. This indiscriminate, capricious picture of God's holy wrath couldn't be more misleading; the subject of substitution couldn't be more mishandled.

The simple fact stands: Forgiveness required the penalty of death. The entire sanctuary service makes this clear. Jesus Himself said at the Last Supper, "This is My blood of the covenant, which is poured out for many *for forgiveness* of sins" (Matthew 26:28, emphasis mine). The flow of God's mercy was obstructed by sin, and only the satisfaction of justice could remove that barrier. Yet far from venting for His own selfish release, God not only discharged, but *absorbed* His justice. Far from being God's scapegoat, Jesus was God's beloved *Son*. The idea of a selfishly anger-venting God is a crass denial of the oneness of the Godhead. The intimacy was so profound that in sending His Son to die, God was sending *Himself*.

Ultimately, God's forgiveness helped inform mine. I had been *overlooking* rather than *forgiving* sin. By denying its seriousness I had actually given it more power. But as the cross revealed the gravity of sin, it also provided a basis for pardon. Because Jesus died, I could forgive my betrayer without enabling. In this way the gospel repairs deep wounds. The concept of forgiveness simultaneously identifies the offense as inexcusable and the offended as merciful. Forgiveness is sober, realistic, honest, and at the same time heals the root of the problem rather than smoothing over the symptoms. True forgiveness creates a workroom where reconciliation can take place. Without creating first that holy space, "reconciliation" is just making nice.

I like to think of reconciliation as a dance (pardon me if you don't like the dance analogy). The steps are forgiveness, forgiveness, trust. That has a nice rhythm, doesn't it? (pardon me if you don't like the rhythm analogy!) Forgiveness, forgiveness, trust. Ahhh, it sounds like a conflict resolved and a relationship healed. The steps to the dance are simple; there are two steps of forgiveness that come before trust is reestablished in a broken relationship.

Forgiveness, step one refers to the one-sided forgiveness of the wronged—a tuning of the spirit and positioning of the will toward mercy. Forgiveness literally means "to send away." This echoes the language of Micah 7:19: "Yes, Thou wilt cast all their sins into the depth of the sea." There is a detachment from the sin, a willing, intentional thrusting away that occurs in forgiveness. This is somehow very different from the denial and enabling that often passes for mercy. With all our talk of accountability and boundaries these days, we can't deny the gospel's call to a posture of pardon toward even unrepentant wrongdoers. For instance:

God is "ready to forgive" (Psalm 86:5), or simply "forgiving."

Jesus said of the Roman soldiers who nailed him to the cross, "Father, forgive them, for they do not know what they do" (Luke 23:34, NKJV). This prayer "embraced the world."[3]

The prayer of the first Christian martyr Stephen was, "Lord, do not charge them with this sin" (Acts 7:60, NKJV).

In Jesus' magnum opus on reconciliation in Matthew 18, the king's forgiveness of the property manager was said to symbolize "divine forgiveness of all sin."[4]

In commenting on this, Ellen White said, "We should not think that unless those who have injured us confess the wrong we are justified in withholding from them our forgiveness. It is their part, no doubt, to humble their hearts by repentance and confession; but we are to have a spirit of compassion toward those who have trespassed against us, whether or not they confess their faults."[5]

From these evidences we see that forgiveness may be one-sided.

We are blessed when we forgive freely. And we can get that blessing before our wrongdoer repents. Mental health professionals know that forgiveness greatly benefits the bestower, improving such conditions as depression, anxiety and even serious personality disorders. This is why these professionals go to great lengths to identify and cultivate attributes that enable a person to forgive. How to persuade people to forgive? they ask. Here is an amazing insight from an enlightening piece of scientific research: "Seeing one's own capability for wrongdoing predicts forgiveness."[6] Did you get that? This study proved that *knowing our sinfulness makes us more forgiving.* Seeing through to the core of our universally selfish hearts, we are induced to release, to "send away" our right to exact revenge upon the perpetrator—for in fact being the victim does give us a certain "right" to take an eye for an eye and a tooth for a tooth.[7]

The perpetrators of wrongdoing themselves benefit from our spirit of forgiveness. Through its prism shines the forgiveness of Jesus, and unless their hearts are stone, this "goodness of God" will draw them toward repentance (see Romans 2:4). Like a warm compress pulls poison out of a snake bite, that "spirit of gentleness" will create an atmosphere conducive to drawing a confession from the one burdened with guilt.

Forgiveness, step two completes what step one began. We might call step one the *objective* phase of forgiveness, and step two the *subjective* phase. Many a wrongdoer never enters into this step and is, subjectively speaking, unforgiven. For instance, the Roman soldiers "by their impenitence would make it an impossibility for the prayer of Christ to be answered *for them.*"[8] Though God was "ready to forgive" these soldiers, their own impenitence prevented it! This is why forgiveness is often presented in "if" terms. 1 John 1:9 says that "*If* we confess our sins, He is faithful and just to forgive us our sins" (NKJV, emphasis mine). Jesus plainly said, "For *if* you forgive others for their transgressions, your heavenly Father will also forgive you. But *if* you do not forgive others, then your Father will not forgive your transgressions," (Matthew 6:14, 15).

So, is God's forgiveness—and ours if we follow His example—conditional or unconditional? Here's how this must work: God's attitude and spirit are forgiveness for all, but He won't forgive bitter, resentful people because He *can't* forgive them. Inflow and outflow of forgiveness use the same channel, which can be blocked by the bile of bitterness. The wronged may forgive from a distance, but there is a frustration of grace while mercy is resisted by the one who needs it. The second step of forgiveness requires a receptivity on the part of the wrongdoer, a recognition of the harm caused, a confession of sin, and restoration when possible. Objective forgiveness may forestall condemnation, yet leave the wrongdoer in an unforgiven state.

This objective/subjective model of forgiveness helped me understand for the first time the issue of blasphemy against the Holy Spirit. As a young Christian, I had encountered a man who claimed he was lost. As he bemoaned his fate, my colleagues and I couldn't help but wonder what he had done. We sat paralyzed and silent because we didn't understand the gospel well enough to offer hope. This experience had always haunted me, but as I began to grasp the truth, I could say with confidence that the only sin that can't be forgiven is the one that isn't available to the Forgiver. No matter how far you've fallen, how egregiously you've sinned, or how low you've stooped, God can forgive you *if you allow Him*.

Trust is the blessed, albeit slow, rebuilding of a broken bond. This step in the dance can't be rushed. While God does require us to forgive wrongdoers, He doesn't require us to trust them. Trust in a relationship can't be exacted; it must be earned.

Confusing forgiveness and trust can prevent forgiveness because the wronged view the process in all-or-nothing terms, thinking, *If I forgive, I'll have to trust again, so I'll stay mad.* Bitterness becomes the only safe option. Don't make this mistake. The dance won't even start if it's hurried!

In fact, victims of abuse who are pressured to bestow unmerited trust often feel as if they are merely going through the motions of a relationship; they have long detached emotionally. Better for them to forgive freely, but let the wrongdoer know that change must come before trust can be reestablished.

To be fair, though, trust is always a risk. Even when evidence shows that trust is well-placed, things go bad. This is why trust is the most delicate, interactive, and detailed step of the dance of reconciliation. The truly repentant will tread lightly, never demanding, but ever firm in their purpose of restoration.

The forgiveness-forgiveness-trust steps we follow in our human relationships are but a reproduction of the divinely-choreographed steps of a God who wants intimate interaction with His children. He took the first step "while we were helpless," "while we were sinners," "while we were enemies." From the Greek, "helpless" implies disabled, "sinners" are literally deviants, and "enemies" indicates active hostility. This all means that before we could or would take a step, and even while we were stepping on Him, Christ took a leap from heaven to hell to save us. He is the great Initiator in the dance of salvation, the leading Man upon Whom we lean and after Whom we follow.

But the second step is taken by two, together. All the forgiveness and grace Jesus poured out for us on the cross won't save us unless it's received. And we won't receive it if we don't first receive godly sorrow which "produces repentance without regret" (2 Corinthians 7:10). All of these things are gifts—we must only come to Him in order to receive them. Once received, forgiveness releases from guilt without the slightest speck of denial. Not a mere legal exchange, forgiveness is a super-charged, transformational, life-altering gift from God, who will also "cleanse us from all unrighteousness" (1 John 1:9).

Finally, restoration of trust takes place. We speak often about trusting God, but do we realize that our need to trust originated in our Creator, in whose image we are made? Does it ever occur to us that God is looking for someone *He* can trust? Does the fact that He took that infinite first step while we were still stepping upon Him move us to dance with Him, obediently and forever?

In Christianity, God seeks elusive man to bestow forgiveness, and man responds with a change of heart toward God.

In legalism, man seeks an elusive God to obtain forgiveness, and God responds with a change of heart toward man.

In Christianity, God begins the process of reconciliation, and man completes it by saying "yes" to God.

In legalism, man begins the process of reconciliation, and God completes it by saying "yes" to man.

Endnotes

1) Card, Michael, "Why?" in his CD, *Brother to Brother*, or *Join the Journey*, 1984, Mole End Music.

2) *Youth's Instructor*, November 29, 1894.

3) *The Desire of Ages*, p. 745.

4) *Christ's Object Lessons*, p. 244.

5) *Thoughts from the Mount of Blessing*, pages 113 and 114.

6) Exline, J. J.; Baumeister, Roy F., et. al. Not So Innocent: Does seeing one's own capability for wrongdoing predict forgiveness? *Journal of Personality and Social Psychology*. Vol. 94(3), Mar 2008, 495-515.

7) See Leviticus 24:20; Deuteronomy 19:21; Exodus 21:23.

8) *Desire of Ages*, p. 745.

Chapter Twelve
A Brief History of Agape

Love and the gospel are partners. An expanded version of this is that wherever the gospel is preached, a pure, uncluttered understanding of God's love shines forth. The humble heart that surrenders to Christ's righteousness also gratefully receives His love.

Many run from God when they have fallen. Just when they need to pray, they stop praying. Like shy babies, they hide their eyes, thinking this will hide *them*, when it only hides the feared object *from* them. They can't shake God's presence, not really; but they think they can, so they bury themselves, thinking, *I'll straighten myself out in private.* There is much that could be said about this, but my point has to do with human nature: This impulse reveals our basic appetite for *deservingness.* Deservingness is a sense of entitlement based on our supposed worthiness. Unlike repentance, deservingness keeps the ego intact. Driven by deservingness, we feel a powerful impulse to fix ourselves before approaching God. We don't naturally want the kind of acceptance that isn't based on our assets—it's too humiliating. This is what causes us to hide our faces when we fall. It keeps us from that horrifying thing called unconditional love.

But deservingness breeds insecurity. We can never quite feel safe from rejection when love and acceptance are on the basis of good performance. What if our performance fails? What if it was never truly good, and our disguise is finally torn away? A deserving person is an insecure person; but happy is the humbled soul who learns to point his fallen feet toward the cross the moment mercy is needed. Happy is the heart that joyfully receives pure, unearned love and forgiveness. Take it from the most undeserving of God's creatures—it's really such a relief.

There is no equal to this undeserved love. John said, "Behold *what manner* of love the Father has bestowed on us" (1 John 3:1, emphasis mine). This love is a specific, distinctive type which we are enjoined to "behold" or examine. The net result of this beholding process is that "when He shall appear, we shall be like Him, for we shall see Him as He is" (1 John 3:2). This special love is therefore very strong medicine, very unique and powerful stuff to create in us Jesus' likeness, preparing us for His coming. The question is raised: how is it different than the love we have known? Conceptualizing it can be difficult, since we have no inborn appreciation of it.

Fortunately, God has made it very simple by putting love in a form we can understand. Love is more than a concept; it's a Person, for "God is love" (1 John 4:16). Because we can't see God directly, He sent Jesus, who "declared" or "explained" God (see John 1:18). Specifically, Jesus was "glorified," or revealed, at the cross (see John 17:1). The love displayed there was supremely self-giving, a flowing-out of the riches of heaven upon the sin-stricken of Earth. Jesus "poured out Himself to death," "for your sake He became poor, that you through His poverty might become rich" (Isaiah 53:12; 2 Corinthians 8:9).

And this is the essential difference. God's love is self-giving; "Love. . .does not seek its own" (1 Corinthians 13:5). Human love, on the other hand, is self-getting, and in ways ranging from subtle and convoluted to blatant and direct, seeks its own. This self-preserving, self-exalting, and self-defending drive is what accounts for the fact that human love rises up in protest against God's love. Unselfish love is, to the selfish heart, a standing rebuke so threatening that it provokes murderous impulses. Thus the phenomenon of the cross—history's most beneficent figure, crucified. We hated Jesus. More specifically, we hated His "manner of love."

Wherever it has resurfaced over the span of history, this self-abnegating, sacrificial, heroic love has been, like the true gospel, a stumbling stone, a *skandalon*, constantly rebuking our egocentricity like Mother Teresa rebukes our materialism. Just as the Person of love suffered attack, the Biblical *idea* of love has been assaulted, directly and subtly, throughout the ages.

In order to understand how this has happened, we need a lesson in linguistics. We'll reference Greek, because Western thought had its origins in Greek culture and philosophy. Greek provides four basic labels for love. In this sense it's far more colorful than English, where we have one word to describe the gamut from heaven's holiest impulse to our taste for Swiss chocolate. Three of the terms describe human love, and one came to be associated with divine love. They are:

Storge - familial love, or specifically the love of a mother for a child.
Phileo - friendship love, or camaraderie.
Eros - romantic, sexual or erotic love.
Agape - God's selfless love.

The relationship divine love sustains to the human loves is like that of a root system to the branches of a plant. It informs and empowers human bonding; it supplies direction as well as strength. Without *agape's* underpinning, the structure of all relationships crumbles, to which the broken human bonds around us attest. The human loves are God-given capacities, but empty, broken shells or unhealthy collusions when not grounded in God.

The enemy's constant effort is therefore to supplant our understanding of God's love with a human counterfeit. If he can blind our minds to *agape*, he can ruin us temporally and eternally. The great controversy between Christ and Satan is also a contention between God's love and Satan's perversions. Because the history of Western religious thought reveals this very vividly, I've mapped out here a brief history of *agape*, a timeline of the concept of love:

Plato was a Greek philosopher who lived and taught four centuries B.C. He is thought to have had a greater impact on Western thought than anyone save Christ Himself. His passion and focus were *eros*—romantic or sexual love—but realizing that this often led to base sensuality, he spiritualized it into non sexual *eros*, often called "platonic" love because of its originator. He described it succinctly: "A god holds no intercourse with man, but by means of this intermediary [spiritual *eros*], all intercourse and discourse between gods and man is carried on."[1] In this redefinition of *eros*, however, it remained unchanged; spiritual *eros* was still a love based on attraction, upon the beauty of the object, and ultimately upon the enrichment of self through the acquirement of that object.

Jesus burst on the scene as the new era dawned, an embodiment of a "new" love that turned the world upside down. Although this love had been taught and demonstrated in ages past, Jesus was that *agape* in undiluted strength. So striking was this love that He wound up crucified for it. *Agape* utterly contrasted with *eros* in that it poured itself out rather than lifting itself up, tumbling from heaven's height to hell itself as Jesus rescued the undeserving.

Augustine was a Catholic teacher whose influence began about three centuries after Christ, during what is called the "great compromise" of Christianity and paganism. This brilliant scholar formed a synthesis between Plato's *eros* and Christ's *agape* and called it "*caritas*" ("charity" in English). In His mind, *eros* and *agape* worked together to save mankind. "Eros is man's longing to get beyond all that is transient and even beyond himself up to the Divine, but the ascent provokes superbia and self-sufficiency, with the result that man remains after all within himself, and never reaches the divine."[2] This confused idea of love helped plunge Europe into the Dark Ages.

Martin Luther and other Reformers reintroduced a God who went from heaven to hell to lift man from his lost estate. Through righteousness by faith the light of *agape* again began to shine. Sinners saw that Christ's love, like His righteousness, is never deserved, but is a free gift bestowed upon the unworthy. Commenting on Martin Luther, the theologian Andres Nygren said, "The very same thing which made him a reformer in the matter of justification, made him also the reformer in the Christian idea of love."[3] What this means is that where the gospel is preached, *agape* will shine.

Ignatius of Loyola, who founded the Jesuit Order beginning in 1560, led in the post-Reformation Catholic revival called the Counter-Reformation. During that period the Catholic Church reestablished its teaching that salvation was by faith *plus* works—not solely faith, as the Reformers taught. Along with human works, human love and self-sacrifice were focused upon and thought to have saving merit. In place of the emotionalism of Augustine, the Jesuits advocated effective (volitional) love rather than affective (emotional) love. This led to great sacrifices as the Jesuits were cut off from earthly ties and interests in stern pursuit of their religion. But impressive as their devotion was, it was in reality a pious veil over a corrupt purpose: "Vowed to perpetual poverty and humility, it was their studied aim to secure wealth and power, to be devoted to the overthrow of Protestantism and the re-establishment of the papal supremacy."[4] This was an ingenious new deception. It was the basest self-exaltation posing as the noblest self-denial.

The pure light of the Protestant Reformation was only temporarily dimmed. It was God's design that the United States, the "lamblike beast" of Bible prophecy, would cradle the gospel's next emergence. The great revivals of early U.S. history indeed put forth the gospel to thousands; but God had an even more dazzling revelation planned. Through the Adventist movement, righteousness by faith would be preached in the context of all ten commandments, thus fulfilling the end-time prophecy, "Here is the patience of the saints. Here are those who keep the commandments of God and the faith of Jesus" (Revelation 14:12). Early Adventism was very astute at the first half of this prophetic equation, but lacking in the last half. Jones and Waggoner were raised up by God to reestablish righteousness by faith, bringing forth the most brilliant revelation yet of God's goodness. That goodness was spelled *A-G-A-P-E*, the uniquely featured love of God for a reprobate and undeserving world:

"Sometimes when a declaration of love is made, the loved one asks, "Why do you love me?" Just as if anybody could give a reason for love! Love is its own reason. If the lover can tell just why he loves another, that very answer shows that he does not really love. . . . Love loves, simply because it is love. Love is the quality of the individual who loves, and he loves because he has love, irrespective of the character of the object."[5]

In the same breath the gospel tells us that salvation and love are undeserved gifts. Just as Jesus saved us when we were sinners, He loved us when we were enemies. Righteousness by faith puts to death our self-righteousness just as agape puts to death our self-exaltation. The result is "unfeigned love of the brethren" (1 Peter 1:22), *koinonia*, or communion, the basis of community. The reception of an undeserved gift opens the human spirit, vertically and horizontally. Love gratefully received from God spills out in love graciously shared with people. Just as a tree receives sunshine and rain from the heavens, so it bears the fruit of the earth.

This is the witness for want of which the world languishes, and the final touch on God's masterpiece of redemption. We fool ourselves when we think proud men do great things—not in the final reckoning, they don't. Not in finishing the gospel work, they don't. The proud may raise up mighty institutions, accomplish extraordinary feats, exercise enormous prowess, publish best-selling books, acquire world renown, display exceptional talent, and even positively impact the lives of millions; but in the face of the task of bringing the everlasting gospel to the world, pride is bankrupt. Put through the echo chamber of heaven, pride-motivated words decay into a noisy-gong-clanging-symbol cacophony. God isn't impressed. Pride-motivated religion will ultimately fail. "Love," on the other hand, "never fails." *Love* is the vehicle through which God will bring the gospel to the world in the fading days of earth's history. *Love* will finish the work.

"Christ is waiting with longing desire for the manifestation of Himself in His church. When the character of Christ shall be perfectly reproduced in His people, then He will come to claim them as His own."[6]

Getting the *idea* of love into *practice* is the next step in the journey.

Endnotes

1) *Symposium* 203, quoted in *Agape and Eros,* Andres Nygren, p. 177.

2) Tract ii. 4., quoted in *Agape and Eros,* Andres Nygren, p. 472.

3) *Agape and Eros,* p. 683.

4) *The Great Controversy,* p. 234.

5) E. J. Waggoner, *The Glad Tidings*, page 116.

6) *Christ's Object Lessons,* p. 69.

Chapter Thirteen
Law ~~and~~ of Love

Where justification by faith is embraced, there is love. Legalism, with all its high and mighty pretentions to holiness, can't replicate this love. In fact, it tends to produce a vexing incongruity between profession and practice. High standards, if not accompanied by compassion and care for people, aren't really high standards; they're a veneer, a coating of gloss on decaying wood.

Over and over the Word distills the law into love:

"A new commandment I give to you, that you love one another, even as I have loved you (John 13:34; see also John 15:12).

"Love does no wrong to a neighbor; love therefore is the fulfillment of the law" (Romans 13:10).

"For the whole law is fulfilled in one word, in the statement, 'You shall love your neighbor as yourself'" (Galatians 5:14).

"By this the children of God and the children of the devil are obvious: anyone who does not practice righteousness is not of God, nor the one who does not love his brother" (1 John 3:10).

"And this is His commandment, that we believe in the name of His Son Jesus Christ and love one another, just as He commanded us" (1 John 3:23).

Here's a little story that illustrates our need for these reminders. During the years I worked with the health ministry I was a prolific songwriter, cranking out one, two, sometimes three songs a week. Before I could record and release the songs, I had to submit them to a committee who screened them for "appropriateness." One song, called "Morning Star" was particularly affective, sensitive, and expressive of my adoration for Jesus. After I played my little song for the tribunal, one individual erupted into a stinging denunciation; "That is the most soppy, sentimental song I've ever heard! No! You can't record that song!" he cried, eyes rolling and arms waving. For several minutes he ranted while I stared, stunned and shamed. Now, it may have been argued that the song was on the sentimental side, but there was no blatant sin in it. On the other hand, his mean-spirited rant was completely out of line. Had Jesus been there, He would have said, "You blind guide[s], who strain at a gnat (a gray, interpretable issue) and swallow a camel (a black-and-white issue, like human dignity)!" (Matthew 23:24, parentheses mine).

How did we get to the place where zeal for "standards" gave us the right to run roughshod over the feelings of others? Does Christianity make a social brute out of a person? Does it make a person less humane than the heathen? Does it make the world a safe refuge from a church filled with emotional terrorists? Does pleasing God mandate indifference to people's self-worth? Absolutely not! The faith of Jesus sensitizes and refines character, increasing rather than decreasing compassion and tenderness.

It is strange but true that Pharisees are the greatest reprobates. Pride in one's law-keeping always results in failure to truly keep the law. This is simply because legalism harbors a spiritual vanity, an egocentric belief in the power and goodness of self. Pride bears fruit in rebellion against God, however concealed that rebellion may be. This is why goody-goody is really baddy-baddy. And this is why Pharisees are the most difficult people to reach; they deflect conviction like corrupt cops.

True obedience is love—not love that contradicts the law, but love that harmonizes with it. The issue is not whether or not the law is our standard. Both legalism and righteousness by faith recognize that the ten-commandment law is the transcendent, authoritative, universal standard of conduct for all humanity. What the two camps disagree on is the *use* of that law. Legalism attempts (however subtly) to use it as a ladder to heaven, while the gospel uses it as evidence that we need the true Ladder, Jesus Christ.

The entire 1888 conflict revolved around the issue of the purpose of the law. Carrying a load of spiritual pride, the "old guard" of Adventism subtly conveyed to their opponents that Sabbath-keeping had merit before God. To this the Sunday-keeping Protestants would cry, "Legalism!" buttressing their charge with such verses as Galatians 3:24: "Wherefore the law was our schoolmaster to bring us unto Christ, that we might be justified by faith." The Adventists would reply that the law in Galatians was the *ceremonial* law rather than the ten-commandment law. They reasoned that Christ obsoleted the former but not the latter, which was still binding. This is all fine, but they evaded the real issue—whether obedience saves us or not. Imagine the shock of the old guard when Jones and Waggoner came upon the scene, arguing that the law in Galatians was the moral law, and that it was *not* contributory to salvation, but only revealed the *need* of salvation. It seemed as if the 1888 messengers were traitors, striking at the very foundation of Adventism.[1] The ensuing polemic has reverberated ever since.

How God and the angels must have laughed and cried simultaneously as they saw these brethren striving over the law rather than living its principle of love. They couldn't have been more self-contradictory if they were bombing abortion clinics. Some of the ugliest politics of Adventist history took place in 1888, as slanderous charges were made, often in the absence of the charged. Unfortunately, it continued into the next millennium and even to the present day—all in the name of the law, and the law is supposed to be love! If only the pioneers had known the love into which the law is ultimately distilled, they would never have resisted the righteousness by faith message. They would have recognized it as part and parcel of true, love-informed obedience.

We will do the same. Adventists have been blessed with a treasure trove of truth, but sometimes the ambassadors of truth forget from whence these gifts came. Subtly, gradually, we forget our own lost condition apart from Christ. Bit by bit we come to the place where the very truths that should humble us actually become a source of pride, and we begin to look down upon those less endowed. Little by little Jesus is nudged out of the picture, and the naked theory of His truth stands alone, as frightening as a walking skeleton. This is the spirit of the Pharisees.

A Christless checklist of facts, a Pharisaical list of dos and don'ts, is worse than useless—it's toxic. An inspired source says, "In all human experience a theoretical knowledge of truth has been proved to be insufficient for the saving of the soul. It does not bring forth the fruits of righteousness. *A jealous regard for what is termed theological truth often accompanies a hatred for genuine truth as made manifest in the life.*"[2] A "jealous regard" for dry theory "often" accompanies an antipathy for living faith! Often! This should make us nervous, if not frantic.

Head knowledge has its place. Jesus admitted to the woman at the well that "salvation is of the Jews," meaning that the Old Testament writings possessed the facts about God. But He quickly added, "An hour is coming, and now is, when the true worshipers shall worship the Father in *spirit and truth*" (John 4:22, 23, emphasis mine). This could be rephrased, "True worshipers will worship the Father with *heart and smart.*" No, God isn't calling us to the empty-headed emotionalism so popular in religion today. But neither is He calling us to the no-less-troublesome opposite, a theory of truth bereft of the love of Jesus. A.T. Jones said:

"One of the characteristics of the last days [is that] people will be *heady*; that is, they have their knowledge in their *heads*. But God wants *hearty* people in these days. Instead of people having the big *head*, he wants them to have a big *heart* . . . there is entirely too much theory among Seventh-day Adventists, and not enough experience of the love of Christ in the heart; too much dogma, and not enough of the Spirit of God."[3]

This headiness is what characterizes Laodicea, the last-day church which claims to be "rich" and in "need of nothing." Jesus says to this arrogant people, "I know your deeds, that you are neither cold nor hot; I would that you were cold or hot" (Revelation 3:15, 16). Religious disciplines hinder Laodicea from indulging in flagrant sin, but they don't give her heaven-borne passion for the gospel. As a result, she's neither anti-God (cold) nor filled with God (hot). She's *for* God, but formally, outwardly, dryly so. Jesus says, "So because you are lukewarm, and neither hot nor cold, I will spit you out of my mouth" (vs. 17). "Spit you out" is literally *vomit*. Do you get what Jesus is saying? It's something like, "I wish you were either whole-hearted worldlings or sold-out saints. Your safe-playing makes me want to throw up!"

The Great Physician then prescribes three things for the malady of Laodicea:

"Gold refined by fire"
"White garments"
"Eye salve"

Essentially the cure for Laodicea is the righteousness by faith message:

Gold is love, God's *agape* love, which always accompanies the proclamation of Christ's righteousness in both concept and demonstration.

White garments are, of course, the righteousness of Jesus instead of our own filthy rags.

Eye salve enables us to see ourselves as we are, which is possible only when we know that God loves us and gives us His righteousness.

To Laodicea Jesus cries, "I give you my love and my righteousness, but I want you to see yourself as you are so that you never return to your own filthy rags, and thus your lukewarm state." Continuing, He requests His rightful place at the heart of the Church: "Behold, I stand at the door and knock; if anyone hears My voice and opens the door, I will come in to him, and will dine with him and he with Me" (vs. 20). Once admitted, the Lifegiver revives a dead institution.

The result of that revival will be *love, agape* love. It will be contemplated, integrated and demonstrated by the Lamb's followers. The most loving company of all time, the Church will evoke the cry, "Who is this who looks forth as the morning, fair as the moon, clear as the sun, awesome as an army with banners?" (Song of Solomon 6:10). Then, instead of being a mere hedge of safety to *protect* us *from* the world, the law of love will be an impetus to *project* us *into* the world, "having the everlasting gospel to preach to those who dwell on the earth" (Revelation 14:6, KJV).

Mahatma Ghandi said to a crowd of church leaders, "When you Christians live as your Master did, all of India will bow down to you."[4] In response to a Christian's effort to convert him, he replied, "From the point of view of sacrifice, it seemed to me that the Hindus greatly surpassed the Christians."[5] In the absence of living, flesh-and-blood proof, the truths of the Bible seem to an onlooking world like a bunch of outlandish claims created to advance the cause of a religious institution. But the message of Christ's righteousness will make a living, breathing movement out of a lukewarm organization.

Believers, it's time to allow God to authenticate our faith. "Search heaven and earth, and there is no truth revealed more powerful than that which is made manifest in works of mercy to those who need our sympathy and aid. This is the truth as it is in Jesus."[6]

The theory of truth "puffs up."

The spirit of truth "lays the glory of man in the dust."

The theory of truth will gratify insiders and frighten outsiders.

The spirit of truth will humble insiders and draw outsiders.

The theory of truth hates the spirit of truth.

The spirit of truth loves the truth completely.

The theory of truth uses truth to elevate itself above fellow sinners.

The spirit of truth feels a humble responsibility toward fellow sinners.

The theory of truth makes us "rich and increased with goods."

The spirit of truth makes us debtors to those who don't know the truth.

The theory of truth rests satisfied with what it has until it has nothing.

The spirit of truth searches for more until it has Everything.

Endnotes

1) Although they really weren't. In a letter written in 1896 Ellen White said, "An unwillingness to yield up preconceived opinions, and to accept this truth, lay at the foundation of a large share of the opposition manifested at Minneapolis."

2) *The Desire of Ages,* p. 309, emphasis mine!

3) A.T. Jones, *General Conference Bulletin,* 1995, p. 173.

4) A personal interview with an eyewitness.

5) *A Ghandi Reader,* p. 36.

6) *Thoughts from the Mount of Blessing,* p. 137.

Chapter Fourteen
The Gospel According to Mary M.

Mary's hands stroke the feet of the Master as thick, sweet rivers run down her wrists and soak into the dirt floor. No one notices her until a fragrance fills the room, which drifts into their consciousness and registers its identity in two phases: "spikenard" first, then "hundreds of denarii, a life savings." In spite of their austere living conditions, the disciples of the One who made Himself poor that they might be made rich still know the smell of money.

Their eyes fall upon the whimpering form on the floor before the Master. They see shards of alabaster, then notice glistening oil all over Him—His beard, face, shoulders, feet. They piece together the facts of this pathetic scene and moan inside themselves with embarrassment.

Judas is the first to speak. His scorn is infused with guilt. "Why this waste?" he asks. "This perfume might have been sold for a high price and the money given to the poor." Mary trembles at the implication that what she thought was devotion was actually foolishness. *Could it be?* She begins to shrink away when suddenly she hears the Voice.

"Leave her alone," He says. "She has done all she could." Mary's tears drop from her hanging head and dot the floor, almost audibly now that the room is stone silent.

A woman? A woman with a past? He has stooped to defend her? The questions hang unanswered except by the obvious. At her knees lay the broken alabaster box, evidence of a love-crime that cost her a year's wages. She is caught in the act of loving God without restraint.

She scans through the motives that led to her offering. He forgave her for years of selling her body. He delivered her from seven devils, hunting her down seven times until she was finally willing to give up everything, even her precious bitterness, because He loved her soul. Love was what she had longed for, and here was One who gave it, a man no less—the real item, not some indulgent counterfeit. She heard Him speak of dying for the sins of the world, and in her sorrow she groped for some way to honor Him. According to the law of Moses, the wages of a prostitute were not to be used as an offering. But she could use those wages to buy a gift, and thus, the alabaster box full of precious ointment. It cost her everything she had.

Then she heard them say that He was soon to be king. *Oh, yes, she thought with joy, then I can honor Him as such.* And so she came, uninvited, to Simon's feast. Out came the box, but when it broke, her heart broke with it as if they were one and the same. A total loss of composure followed; a wet face contorted with emotion, a body shaken by sobbing, an irrepressible display of affection. The sweet aroma filled the room the way He had filled her soul, but with this difference: Her offering provoked shame in them, while His offering provoked praise in her. The scent of love has a way of dividing the world into two classes.

Now the Voice was defending her in the presence of those who would turn her out onto the street if they could. He tells them that her act is to be proclaimed wherever His gospel is preached. Again, stunned, stone silence. The implication is too much for Judas. He is smarting with the rebuke, long-held antipathy smoldering in his eyes. He broods... *Can He commend this waste of a human being and in the process censure me?* The spirit is contagious until Simon's eyes catch the same glare. *Doesn't He know what a vile thing she is? Why does He let her touch Him?*

Mary smarts under the injustice. The very one who ruptured her innocence thinks himself superior to his victim. It isn't the first time the perpetrator has triumphed over the prey, and it won't be the last. But she has tasted this bitter irony too long. *Let it go, let it go.* She is pure again; she knows it. *Feel pity for him who doesn't.*

Now the Voice speaks a parable. Two debtors, one owing ten times more. Both forgiven. "Who," He asks, "should love the most?"

"The one whom he forgave the most," Simon mutters, knowing in that instant that he is apprehended. The sweat glands in this guilty one's face explode, paling him to a gray-white. It is as if a supernatural Glance has pierced his skin and inspected the secret rooms of his soul—the dark, defensive rooms where there is no light, no air. As the Eyes probe, he feels a flicker of despair and corresponding rage. He is ready to retreat into his secret room again, to slam the door to the light, when he sees something in the Eyes that arrest him. They are more than omniscient and omnipotent. They are omnibenevolent. They are all-love. *All* love.

A wonder comes to pass. Reality comes rushing into Simon's consciousness. He understands that Jesus knows his great sin; Yet He does not expose nor shame him. Time warps for a moment as love and sin meet face to face. Sin disintegrates and love triumphs. For the first time since he ruined his life and hers, Simon feels safe to break into a million fragments. He who could have snapped in brittleness shatters in remorse. He casts a glance at Mary, the living monument of his shame. Suddenly, she is the powerful one and he the suppliant. *Would she forgive him too?* The humble slant of her shoulders, the grateful sorrow on her face, speak *yes, yes, she will.*

Impossible healing has begun.

The spectacle unfolds. The broken box has marked its trail, and the ensuing river of grace will flow over all that it touches. For ages to come it will be told—the story of this broken woman and her broken box. Here are the first-fruits of the power of her witness, the ability of God working through a human heart to flip the misery of sin on its axis and make that very sin an opportunity to prove grace. Mary was Simon's victim. Simon is Mary's convert. Love was crucified by humanity. Humanity is saved by Love. What win-win transaction is better than the great exchange?

For a moment in time, Mary Magdalene was a mirror of Christ. Her worship was so pure, so selfless, that He could point to her act and know that He would shine through it. He did not say that her deed should be proclaimed "wherever this gospel is preached" because it would supplement or garnish the gospel story, but because it would authenticate, affirm, and reinforce it. In commanding that her story be told side by side with His, He was saying, "Mary's act of sacrifice and mine are of the same character. She has echoed without words the Word I have spoken. Her actions have reflected my gospel. My story shows what I did *for* people, Mary's story shows what I can do *in* people. Look at her and you will see Me."

Mary was also a prototype of the bride of Christ. Someday, a people will reflect Him so completely that He will be able to showcase them before the world, knowing that the world will see only Him. It will not be mere technological advances that finally spread the message of the gospel to every living creature; it will be love personified. God will know when His people are ready, and He will arrange the lights, camera, and action when the time is right.

Does it seem presumptuous to say that sinners can ever reflect a holy God so fully? The story of Mary Magdalene gives evidence that it is not, for Jesus Himself would then be presumptuous. He was the One who commanded that attention be given to her deed, to glorify not man, but God. Why else would He give her such prime-time exposure? Consider these predictions:

"Wherever this gospel is preached *in the whole world,* what this woman has done will also be told as a memorial to her" (Matthew 26:13, NKJV, emphasis mine).

"This gospel of the kingdom will be preached *in all the world* as a witness to all the nations, and then the end will come" (Matthew 24:14, NKJV, emphasis mine).

"Go *into all the world* and preach the gospel to every creature" (Mark 16:15, NKJV, emphasis mine).

Someday every living inhabitant of the earth—the whole world—will have heard the gospel. They will also have heard about Mary. Refine that a little further. The focal point of the gospel, even the gospel itself, is the cross. This means that someday every man, woman, and child will know about two acts of self-giving love: Christ's and Mary's.

What was it about Mary's gift of precious ointment that reflected Heaven's Gift of the spotless Son? They were both:

Far-reaching:

Christ's cross was "an offering and a sacrifice to God for a sweet-smelling *aroma*" (Ephesians 5:2, NKJV, emphasis mine).

Mary's gift was "a pound of very costly oil of spikenard. . . . And the house was filled with the *fragrance* of the oil" (John 12:3, NKJV, emphasis mine).

Precious:

Christ's cross was where we were "redeemed . . . with the *precious* blood of Christ" (1 Peter 1:18,19, NKJV, emphasis mine).

Mary's ointment was "very costly" and "might have been sold for more than three hundred denarii" (Mark 14:3, 5, NKJV). One denarii was about a day's wages (see Matthew 20:2), making Mary's purchase worth about a year's wages.

Extravagant:

Christ's cross was a seeming waste, but "*it could not be restricted* so as not to exceed the number who would accept the great gift."[1]

Mary's gift likewise seemed like a squandering of resources and provoked the words, "Why this *waste*?" (Matthew 26:8, emphasis mine).

Ridiculed:

Christ's cross hung in the midst of mocking rulers, Romans soldiers, and people. Jesus was "a reproach of men, and despised of the people." He said, "All those who see Me ridicule Me" (Psalm 22:6, 7, NKJV).

Mary's gift brought the same scorn, for "when His disciples saw it, they were indignant" (Matthew 26:8, NKJV).

Permanent:

Christ's cross gave Him wounds that will always remain, significant of His eternal identification with humanity. (see John 20:27; Zechariah 13:6.)

Mary's gift was contained in an alabaster box that, once broken, could never be resealed.[2]

Converting:

Christ's cross induced Simon of Cyrene to "take the cross from choice";[3] the thief on the cross to say, "Lord, remember me when You come into Your kingdom" (Luke 23:42, NKJV); the Roman soldier to say, "Truly this was the Son of God!" (Matthew 27:54, NKJV).

Mary's gift led to the conversion of Simon, who "became a lowly, self-sacrificing disciple."[4]

Disaffecting:

Christ's cross led to the Jewish nation's complete rejection of God when they cried, "We have no king but Caesar" (John 19:15).

Mary's gift led to Judas's complete rejection of Christ, for "from the supper he went directly to the palace of the high priest, where he . . . offered to betray Christ into their hands."[5]

Drawing:

Christ's cross will draw "a great multitude, which no one could count," who will "[stand] before the throne and before the Lamb" (Revelation 7:9).

Mary's gift would "shed its fragrance" wherever the gospel was preached, and "until time should be no more, that broken alabaster box would tell the story of the abundant love of God for a fallen race."[6]

Faith-led:

Christ's cross was the pinnacle of His expression of the love of God, which He brought to us through utter darkness when "By faith, Christ was the victor."[7] "The faith of Jesus" is a faith that works "through love" (Revelation 14:12; Galatians 5:6, NKJV).

Mary's gift was a response of gratitude to the love of Jesus for her soul. Jesus said, "Your faith has saved you; go in peace" (Luke 7:50).

There is more. The church will reflect Jesus one day. A whole army of Mary Magdalenes will arise out of the swamp of humanity, bearing the lily-white righteousness of Christ. Our offerings can never equal the pattern of Calvary, but they can follow it. Jesus was unafraid to draw attention to what Mary did, and He is still in search of those through whom He can shine without obstruction:

"The church is the depositary of the wealth of the riches of the grace of Christ, and through the church eventually will be made manifest the final and full display of the love of God to the world that is to be lightened with its glory" (TTM 50).

In the beginning of the war, Satan declared that justice destroyed mercy, that sin could not be forgiven. When the cross disproved this claim, Satan asserted that mercy destroyed justice, that the death of Christ had changed God's law. This charge still lingers in the air, and it can be refuted only by the witness of God through His people. They will prove the immutability of the law by obeying it. Right down to the substrata of their beings, the law of love will be written. Through their living testimony God will declare the perfect harmony between mercy and justice, a harmony Satan has passionately sought to obscure.

Once the proclamation of the third angel's message reaches every ear, the line will be drawn between the true and false gospel, between God's law and man's, between selfless love and self-love, between liberty and coercion. No changes of mind will take place after Jesus shouts, "It is done!" The great experiment of sin will have proven it to be wholly detestable, and God to be wholly worthy of worship and adoration. The faith of God that sinners and sin would be forever separated will bear fruit in that reality. Finally, a people will mirror His cross, which will lighten the earth with His glory.

Endnotes

1) *The Desire of Ages*, p. 566.

2) *Ibid.*, p. 559.

3) *Ibid.*, p. 742.

4) *Ibid.*, p. 568.

5) *Ibid.*, p. 564.

6) *Ibid.*, p. 563.

7) *Ibid.*, p. 756.

Also available from Jennifer Schwirzer:

Testimony of a Seeker - Jennifer's spiritual autobiography.
I Want it All - A creatively-written teen devotional.
Dying to be Beautiful - Help for those suffering from eating disorders.
A Deep but Dazzling Darkness - Written with Leslie Kay on the "dark side"
                                       of God's character.
Finding My Way in Milwaukee - Jennifer's testimony, written for pre-teens.
Healing Inner Wounds - Lecture series on Biblical psychology and healing.
Love in the Last Days - Lecture series on God and human relationships.

Musical Recordings:

Love/Life
Scrapbook
From the Garden to the Cross
Chance of Rain
Hey, Everybody, Good News!
Banish the Myth
Soldier of Hearts

For these and other products, visit our website at **www.jenniferjill.org**.
Jennifer's blog is at **www.jenpenn.com**.